On the Threshold of the Future

On the Threshold of the Future

*The Life and Spirituality
of Mother Mary Joseph Rogers*

Founder of the Maryknoll Sisters

Claudette LaVerdiere, MM

ORBIS BOOKS

Maryknoll, New York 10545

Founded in 1970, Orbis Books endeavors to publish works that enlighten the mind, nourish the spirit, and challenge the conscience. The publishing arm of the Maryknoll Fathers and Brothers, Orbis seeks to explore the global dimensions of the Christian faith and mission, to invite dialogue with diverse cultures and religious traditions, and to serve the cause of reconciliation and peace. The books published reflect the views of their authors and do not represent the official position of the Maryknoll Society. To learn more about Maryknoll and Orbis Books, please visit our website at www.maryknollsociety.org.

Published by Orbis Books, Maryknoll, New York 10545-0302.
Manufactured in the United States of America.
Manuscript editing and typesetting by Joan Weber Laflamme.

Library of Congress Cataloging-in-Publication Data

LaVerdiere, Claudette.
    On the threshold of the future : the life and spirituality of Mother Mary Joseph Rogers, founder of the Maryknoll Sisters / Claudette LaVerdiere.
        p. cm.
    Includes bibliographical references (p.   ) and index.
    ISBN 978-1-57075-942-0 (pbk. : alk. paper) 1. Mary Joseph, Mother, 1882-1955. 2. Maryknoll Sisters. I. Title.
    BX4705.M423L38 2012
    271'.97—dc22
    [B]

                                                              2011010634

In memory of Sister Barbara Hendricks,
beloved Sister and revered leader,
woman of contemplative wisdom
and prophetic vision.

Contents

Foreword   ix
Preface   xiii

Part I
A Short Life of Mother Mary Joseph Rogers

1. The Early Years   3
2. From "Secretaries" to Women Religious   12
3. The Field Afar   21
4. A Community for Mission   27
5. Last of the Founders   34
6. World War II, 1941–1945   38
7. God Has Yet a Great Work for Us to Do   42
8. As One Lamp Lights Another   48
9. Epilogue   50

Part II
Foundations of
Mother Mary Joseph's Mission Vision

10. The American Foreign Mission Context at the Turn
    of the Twentieth Century   55
11. The Catholic Awakening   61
12. Mollie's Path to Maryknoll   64
13. Mother Mary Joseph Rogers's Mission Vision   67

Part III
The Spirituality of
Mother Mary Joseph Rogers

14. The Presence of God   77
15. Contemplation and Action   83
16. Unity of Spirit and Diversity of Gifts   89
17. Individuality and Common Good   97
18. The Maryknoll Spirit of Obedience   104

Contents

19. Nobility of Soul   111
20. *Ecce Ancilla Domini*   115

Chronology of the Life of Mother Mary Joseph Rogers   121
Notes   129
Bibliography   153
Index   155

Foreword

JANICE MCLAUGHLIN, MM

Anniversaries are times to look to the past with gratitude and to the future with hope. Certainly one hundred years provides a unique opportunity to explore the history of our founder, Mary Josephine (Mollie) Rogers, later to be known as Mother Mary Joseph.

Sister Suzanne Noffke, OP, suggests that doing history is in fact "sacramental remembrance" in that the stories from the past can "form and transform us now, to shape our present into the future."[1] In this spirit Sister Claudette LaVerdiere, building on the foundation laid by Sister Barbara Hendricks, has performed a sacred ministry. She has not only documented the life of our founder, but she has also probed the meaning behind her vision of mission and the spiritual wisdom that she shared with the early women who joined her and those who would follow in subsequent generations.

As we search for the meaning that this history has for us today, I suggest that this volume offers new insights into the twentieth-century missionary endeavor among American Catholic women as well as the changing role of women in church and society. The last section, containing the elements of Mollie's spirituality for mission, is rich in insights that are contemporary in their meaning and expression.

Roots of Maryknoll Sisters

Mary Josephine's early life in a middle-class Boston Irish Catholic family may not seem the breeding ground for an international outlook, yet it offers some clues to the unique path that she chose to follow later in life. LaVerdiere traces Mollie's family history, pointing out the people and the events that helped to shape her. Immigration to the United States from eastern and northern Europe was at its peak when Mollie was growing up at the end of the nineteenth and the beginning of the twentieth centuries. More than twelve million immigrants passed through Ellis Island between 1892 and 1924. Irish Catholics were an oppressed minority when Mollie was born and continued to be looked down on until the mid-twentieth century, when the Catholic school system gave them skills that enabled them to climb out of poverty.

Although better off than many immigrants, the Rogers family was aware of the discrimination against the Irish and the challenges that new waves of immigrants brought to this nation. This recognition may have influenced Mollie's attitudes toward those of other cultures. Her choice of tolerance as the theme of her graduation address from high school is an indication of her openness toward those who were different and of her awareness of the problems they faced. It is perhaps no coincidence that the first mission undertaken by Maryknoll Sisters in 1920 was to Japanese immigrants on the West Coast of the United States. Today, Maryknoll Sisters in Japan minister to migrants from the Philippines, who number more than one million. Work with refugees, displaced people, and immigrants continues to be a priority wherever we are.

This book gives us an insight into Mollie's ideas of community life, which were obviously shaped by her experience of a large and loving family that took time to celebrate together and have fun. The tradition of simplicity nights, a kind of amateur hour that is a treasured part of almost every Maryknoll gathering, most likely found its origin in the sing-alongs that took place around the piano in the Rogers' front parlor. The tradition of having ice cream sodas on St. Teresa's Day and special meals for feast days can easily be traced to Mollie's love of cooking and her enjoyment of a good meal around a crowded table of family and friends.

The most obvious influence on Mollie's subsequent life choices was her education at Smith College, an interdenominational institute of higher learning for women that was founded in 1875 to prepare young women for leadership positions in church and society. Women were still second-class citizens in the United States when Mollie was a student, barred from voting and holding public office, and expected to marry and raise a family.

This biography captures the influence of the Protestant missionary movement on Mollie, especially the experience of her classmates being commissioned to serve as missioners in China. This turning point in Mollie's life led her to the office of James Anthony Walsh, the director of the Society for the Propagation of the Faith in Boston. Their collaboration on mission education through the publication of *The Field Afar* magazine was the forerunner of the Maryknoll mission movement with Walsh as the co-founder of the Maryknoll Society of Fathers and Brothers in 1911.

The Role of Women

Although Mollie never uses feminist language and is traditional in some of her attitudes about obedience to church authorities, this volume makes clear that she aspired to a greater role for women in the church than was common at that time. Because she viewed women as equals to men in the mission field, she sent her Sisters to China to do primary evangelization.

Subsequent generations of Maryknoll women have been inspired by this example of going out in teams of two to live among the people and share their daily routine while imparting the gospel message. In 2010, two of our newest Maryknoll Sisters from Indonesia and Vietnam followed in the footsteps of these pioneers as they began language studies in China. Two other members, from Zimbabwe and the United States, joined an integrated community-health project in Haiti in 2011. The tradition that Mollie started is still very much alive.

She also accepted women from other nations and cultures to become Maryknoll Sisters long before this was the case in other American congregations. In recent years vocations to the Maryknoll Sisters from Tanzania, the Philippines, Korea, and other countries in which we work are the norm rather than the exception.

We learn from this book that Mother Mary Joseph had no blueprint for the community of women she led and did not subscribe to a regimental model of religious life that attempted to form all members in the same mold. Rather, she believed that our missionary vocation required a freedom of spirit and movement that raised some eyebrows in her time and continues to do so today. LaVerdiere makes clear that Mollie balanced her desire for us to maintain our individuality with a call for commitment to the common good.

The third section of this book contains some of the deepest insights into the roots of a spirituality that would ground and anchor active missioners in the midst of many demands and hardships. The account of her visitation to China only a few years after the first Sisters went there is very revealing. Not only did she experience the poverty and misery of the local population, but she was also present during a time of political and social turmoil when gangs of bandits often caused the work to cease. She realized that only an awareness of the presence of

God in daily life could enable the Sisters to overcome their fear and accept the hardships. Violence is a growing phenomenon in every one of the twenty-six nations in which our members work today. Mollie's spiritual wisdom is as relevant as ever if we are to persevere in such dangerous and difficult places as El Salvador, Zimbabwe, and Myanmar, to name but three.

LaVerdiere is at her best when she describes the two cornerstones of our mission spirituality—"the presence of God and contemplation in action." Although laden with traditional terms and concepts, Mollie displays a mystical consciousness that is reminiscent of some of the great spiritual masters that so inspired her, such as Teresa of Avila, Thérèse of Lisieux, John of the Cross, and Dominic, as well as Mary, mother of God, whom she held up as a model of generosity and readiness to do God's will. Her insistence on the need to cultivate an awareness of the presence of God in the midst of an active apostolate marks her as the contemplative in action that she urged her Sisters to be.

This unique combination of church history, women's studies, spirituality, and biography is a gift not only to Maryknollers but to all who wish to understand the foundation and inspiration for modern mission. As you read this labor of love, it is well to recall that we do not look to the past to glorify it or to return to it. Rather, we seek to discover the original inspiration and essential elements from which the future will be born. We are grateful that the work begun by Barbara Hendricks and completed by Claudette LaVerdiere has provided us with such a wealth of priceless information and analysis that can help us discover the essence of mission in the twenty-first century and beyond.

Preface

The Maryknoll Sisters Congregation celebrates its one-hundredth anniversary on January 6, 2012. As religious congregations go, that is a relatively short time. During those years only one popular full length biography of Mother Mary Joseph's life has been published: *Maryknoll's First Lady*, by Sister Jeanne Marie Lyons (1964).[1] This book was followed in 1980 by Sister Camilla Kennedy's doctoral dissertation, *To the Uttermost Parts of the Earth: The Spirit and Charism of Mary Josephine Rogers*.[2] Sister Camilla's foundational study gathers together all the important documents for the Maryknoll Sisters' study and reflection on their founder's vision and spiritual legacy. In addition, Penny Lernoux's 1993 oral history of the Maryknoll Sisters, *Hearts on Fire*,[3] provides an inspirational dimension to the holy life of Mother Mary Joseph and the extraordinary deeds she engendered.

A centennial offers an unprecedented opportunity to elaborate further on the significance of a founder's life and spirit. In 1943, Mother Mary Joseph expressed the hope that "somebody, someday . . . [would] write and give us that spirit which certainly ought to be handed-down."[4] Fifty years later, in 1993, Sister Barbara Hendricks began painstakingly to research the rich facets of Mother Mary Joseph's spirituality.[5] She wrote seven essays that she used in retreats to the Sisters at Maryknoll and in our missions throughout the world. The genuinely gracious response of the Sisters moved her to propose writing a short biography of Mother Mary Joseph and to add it to the essays for publication. The Maryknoll Sisters Leadership Team recognized the value of Barbara's work and requested that she write a longer biography. Before Barbara could complete that work to her satisfaction, illness overtook her and the project was passed on to me.

Barbara had directed her account of Mother Mary Joseph's life to the Maryknoll Sisters. The Leadership Team asked me to redo the work in view of a wider readership and to shorten the biographical section, which was precisely what Barbara had originally intended. When I began work on the manuscript, Barbara and Camilla Kennedy, Barbara's good friend and adviser, met with me periodically to assess my progress and give direction to the work. Although Barbara understood the task involved in shortening the text at one point she could not help but express her dismay: "You're taking out all the good parts!"[6] I sincerely hope that in the process of shortening the text, I have not omitted too many of those "good parts" or anything vitally important.

The framework of this short life is entirely Barbara's, and much of her phrasing appears intact. I would like to be able to share that with her, but she died on October 12, 2010, a month before the completion of this work. Barbara not only provided the framework for this text but also the inspiration. She poured her heart and soul into this project so that future generations of Maryknoll Sisters would experience the love, the spiritual depth, and the gracious good humor of their founder.

This volume consists of three parts. The first tells the story of Mother Mary Joseph Rogers, the woman who founded the Maryknoll Sisters Congregation. Part II examines the foundations of her response to the need for mission work. I set this material apart specifically to contextualize the founding of Maryknoll within the events at the turn of the twentieth century. Part III consists of seven themes of Mother Mary Joseph's spirituality. Barbara's seven essays could not simply be appended to this work because, like the biographical section, they were written for the Maryknoll Sisters and would have required a thorough rewriting for a broader readership. Rather than risk losing Barbara's essays, I sought instead to develop several of the binary oppositions Barbara identified in Mother Mary Joseph's writings at the end of her sixth essay: contemplation and action, unity and diversity, individuality and common good, fearless honesty and compassion, and joy and suffering.[7]

Other themes arose from my own reading of Mother Mary Joseph's writings: the presence of God, the Maryknoll spirit of obedience, nobility of soul, and *Ecce Ancilla Domini.*[8] While each of the themes reflects something of Mother Mary Joseph's spirituality, they do not constitute the "last word." In the years to come Maryknoll Sisters will continue to reflect on the writings of Mother Mary Joseph and arrive at new insights. We know that we have not plumbed the depths of Mother Mary Joseph's charism, spirit, or spirituality.

Like Barbara, I, too, have presented these themes in retreats for Maryknoll Sisters and also one for Full Circle members.[9] I, too, have been blessed, not only with very good reception of the material, but always with excellent suggestions for improvement. The themes are, after all, about a revered founder's vision, what she held of the essence for her beloved community.

Finally, I would like to express my gratitude to my Sisters of Maryknoll who accompanied me in prayer and constantly remained interested in this project. I have already mentioned Sisters Barbara and Camilla, whose mentoring early on was a most precious gift. Sisters Anna Maria Hartman and Bernice Kita read early drafts of the thematic essays and made invaluable suggestions. As the project was nearing completion, Sisters Betty Ann Maheu and Nonie Gutzler, together with Bernice Kita, applied their editorial expertise to the entire manuscript. I also thank Ms. Ellen Pierce, director of Maryknoll's Mission Archives, and the staff members who gave unstintingly of their time and effort to locate materials, no matter how obscure.

I started this work in late 2003, with the blessing of Sister Suzanne Moore's Leadership Team, expecting that the book would be completed by the end of its term in 2008. However, due to extenuating circumstances, my work continued into the term of the succeeding team under Sister Janice McLaughlin's presidency. Her Leadership Team extended the blessing and, along with many Sisters, urged me forward. Thanks to their encouragement, this small tribute to Mother Mary Joseph Rogers is making a timely debut on the eve of the Maryknoll Sisters' centennial. May the celebration of her life and spirit inspire many to dedicate their lives to the mission of Jesus in the twenty-first century.

Part I

A Short Life of
Mother Mary Joseph Rogers

1

The Early Years

"Who knows but that the little work we do here may be the beginning of greater efforts in later life."[1] These words, written by Mary Josephine Rogers to Father James Anthony Walsh in 1906, were prophetic, as was his reply: "I believe [this work] will be of far-reaching importance, more so than you realize at the present moment."[2] Neither was aware that this correspondence was the beginning of an ever-deepening friendship that would culminate in Maryknoll, a name synonymous with world mission in the Catholic world. Nor, at that point, could Mary Josephine have imagined the shape or nature of the organization—the Maryknoll Sisters' Congregation—that would evolve in partnership with the Catholic Foreign Mission Society of America—the Maryknoll Fathers and Brothers.

Born in Boston on October 27, 1882, Mary Josephine, or Mollie, as she was affectionately called by family and friends, was the fourth child and the first daughter in a family of eight children. Her father, Abraham, was the youngest of the three surviving sons of Patrick Henry Rogers[3] and Mary Dunn.[4]

Mollie's grandfather, Patrick Henry, had emigrated from Ireland to St. John, New Brunswick, and in 1844, a year after marrying Mary, immigrated to Boston. "The Rogers were known for their brains and strong personalities. Most Irish immigrants had strong men or strong women; the Rogers family had both. They were not only strong personalities; they liked other people with strong personalities and often married people with strong personalities."[5] Patrick Henry and Mary were the perfect exemplars. Patrick could hold his own anywhere in Boston, and Mary was never in his shadow.[6]

Although loyal Roman Catholics, the elder Rogers adroitly accommodated to the Protestant Yankee establishment, and they prospered.[7] They educated their children in public schools to afford them every possible opportunity to thrive at a time when Catholics in Boston were regarded, at best, as second-class citizens. Mollie's father, Abe, graduated from French Commercial College and initially followed his father into the family real-estate business before moving into building construction. Also like his father, he served on the Boston Common Council of 1880 and 1881. In mid-1882, he resigned in order to accept the position of assistant building inspector of West Roxbury. All three of the Rogers' sons were successful in their businesses and through sound financial investments provided for their large, closely bonded families.

The family of Mollie's mother, Josie Plummer, the daughter of an Irish Catholic woman, Bridget Josephine Kennedy, and an eighth-generation Congregationalist Yankee, William Gardner Plummer, personally experienced anti-Catholic discrimination. Although William married Bridget in a Catholic ceremony, he was adverse to his wife's religious practices and would not allow their children to be baptized as Catholics. For this sacrament as well as for others, Bridget had to make surreptitious arrangements. Josie retained the painful memory of having had to "hide" in a neighbor's house to get dressed for her first holy communion.

Following the established tradition in the Rogers clan, Abe and Josie sent all their children, three daughters and five sons, to public schools in Jamaica Plain. After eighth grade one child after the other attended West Roxbury High School. Mollie was self-confident and responsible as an adolescent. She did well in her studies and participated fully in extracurricular activities. Her younger siblings remained attached to her because she was so much fun. The older boys also counted on her to mediate for them with their father when it came to choosing their careers and pursuing their own interests. Within the family Mollie had ample opportunities to hone her natural skills for negotiating potentially conflictive situations.

In the late nineteenth century, when Catholics in the United States had little awareness of world mission, Abe and Josie ensured through Sunday school that their children would grow up with some familiarity of the church's foreign mission activity. Some time in the early 1940s Mollie, now Mother Mary Joseph, made notes of her recollections:

> I cannot remember a time when I was not deeply interested in the people of other lands as well as my own America. I was fortunate, as a child, in having dolls dressed in the costumes of foreign children and in possessing books about Europe, Asia, and Africa, which my parents read to me so that I was, from an early age, keenly alive to the existence of little sisters and brothers in far off lands quite different from myself in race, color and creed. . . . This consciousness

might have developed into a purely social or economic altruism, had not my parents been interested in the Society for the Propagation of the Faith and the Holy Childhood Association . . . the two great agencies in the Catholic Church for collecting funds to help priests and sisters working in the foreign mission fields. . . .

And, as a Catholic child, I was taught to pray for . . . missioners and the children they were trying to teach about God, and to share with them the little store of money that was mine to spend as I liked. Being highly imaginative, I even visualized myself as a missionary going about doing good and converting whole cities. . . .

As I grew older, the day dreams faded, and beyond prayers and small contributions, I paid little heed to the souls for whom our Divine Savior thirsted. It was only in later years, when I was at college and witnessed the activity of my friends in foreign mission work, that the dreams of my youth became real.[8]

With this kind of background Mollie began her college studies at Smith in Northampton, Massachusetts, in the fall of 1901. Although she had wanted to become a nurse, her father insisted she go to college. It is not known how she managed this difference of opinion, but she evidently settled happily into student life at Smith.

Almost from her first day at Smith, her early openness to the world and the peoples of the world was rekindled. The faith her parents had nurtured in her as a child blossomed in the encounters she had with fellow students. One of them questioned her one day about where she went in the mornings. To mass, she replied, and yes, she really believed God came to her every morning in holy communion. The student responded with a sudden rush of tears—if only she could believe that![9] Not one to take her faith for granted, Mollie pondered these experiences, sensing that something would be required of her.

It would not be until a full year after graduating from Smith that a direct challenge from a faculty member would recall with sudden urgency the pledge she had made on a balmy June evening in 1904 at the end of her third year.[10] She had just witnessed the vibrant "mission sending" of the Protestant Student Volunteer Movement. "Something—I do not know how to describe it—happened within me," and she proceeded directly to St. Mary's Church. Kneeling before the Blessed Sacrament, she pledged herself to the mission of the church, having no idea how she might follow through on this commitment. She simply believed that Divine Providence would show the way.

Mollie returned for her last year of college in the fall of 1904, still pondering where God was leading her. While the record contains nothing of her extracurricular activities during her final year, her emerging apostolic energy did not escape the notice of Paulist Father John Handly, who gave a mission for the Catholic students at Smith that year. "When Miss Rogers was in her senior year, she was the leader and sustaining spirit of an organization of Catholic students." He specified that Mollie's group promoted frequent reception of the sacraments, generosity to Catholic missions, and involvement of Catholic students at Smith in what was called Christian work.[11]

Mollie graduated from Smith in June 1905, and a year later, in the fall of 1906, she returned to her alma mater as a demonstrator in zoology, quite unaware of the concern of some faculty members for the Catholic students. While the college offered about twenty Bible study clubs and sponsored as many Protestant mission study clubs, there was nothing comparable for Catholics, who tended to be marginalized from the college's socio-religious activities.[12] Miss Elizabeth Deering Hanscom, faculty adviser of the Smith College Association for Christian Work,[13] sensed that Mollie might be the right person to change this equation. Early in the first term Elizabeth invited Mollie to tea and urged her to do something for the Catholic girls, "perhaps a Bible class." Mollie demurred. She knew little about the Bible (in those days it was unusual for Catholics to study the Bible). However, Mollie instinctively recognized the value of such an undertaking and countered with a suggestion of her own—"How about a mission study club?"—and it was settled.[14]

On the way back to her residence hall, Mollie, not altogether sure of herself, was so unnerved by this commitment that she nearly changed her mind. She knew there were few resources available, and she would need a lot of material—if indeed, she would be able to gather a group of Catholic girls in a mission study club at all! In this frame of mind she consulted Father Welch, her confessor and curate at St. Mary's Church,[15] probably half-hoping he would dissuade her. Instead, he encouraged her to contact Father James Anthony Walsh, director of the Society for the Propagation of the Faith in Boston. Walsh responded enthusiastically to her letter and arranged a meeting for December of that year. Just as she was about to take her leave, he said to her, "I think that you and I are going to be friends."[16] Years later, when Mother Mary Joseph spoke about this incident, she recognized the gracious hand of God in her life. In a moment of fervor in 1904 she had committed herself to the mission of the church. And now, with Father Walsh, her world was beginning to expand in startling new ways. In that first meeting she learned firsthand about his deep desire to awaken American Catholics to their responsibilities in the foreign mission work of the church.

In the months ahead Mollie volunteered her time to translate manuscripts for the mission magazine, *The Field Afar*, recently started by Father Walsh, and to prepare them for publication. She managed this along with her obligations at Smith and the successful initiation of the mission study class.[17] Upon completing her second year as a demonstrator, she transferred to a Boston city school, primarily to collaborate with Walsh on a daily basis.

The work on behalf of foreign missions totally supplanted Mollie's desire for a master's degree in zoology. Her earlier intention to pursue further education had been in line with her father's ambitions. Just as he had more or less intervened in the careers of his sons, he had very specific ideas about the futures of his daughters. As one might expect, when she changed her course in life, she met with a fair amount of resistance.[18] Although Mollie prevailed, working it out certainly demanded exceptional ingenuity. In the years to come, however, she would be gratified by her father's pride in her achievements.[19]

Mollie's reliability and skills as a writer, translator, and editor enabled Walsh to devote more of his energies to pursuing his plans to set up a foreign mission seminary in America. Two chance meetings with a priest from North Carolina, Father Thomas Frederick Price, were critical for the realization of his ideas. In the first meeting, in 1904, he learned that in his native state Father Price was striving to foster a more dynamic missionary thrust. The second encounter was on September 10, 1910, at the International Eucharistic Congress in Montreal. Walsh and Price realized that they indeed shared a common goal: to develop a foreign mission seminary in the United States. Mollie Rogers had been following this unfolding closely. A few days later, on September 15, she privately consecrated her whole life to the foreign mission movement they envisioned.

The year 1910 was one of sea change for James Anthony Walsh, Thomas Frederick Price, and Mary Josephine Rogers, with all three collaborating in pursuit of the same dream. Together, they dedicated their lives to the foundation of a society for foreign missions in the United States. Together, they founded the Maryknoll Mission Movement.

After the meeting in Montreal, Fathers Walsh and Price had seven months to draft a proposal for the approval of the U.S. bishops, who were scheduled to meet in April. The two worked closely with Cardinal James Gibbons, and they called on many bishops personally in order to present their idea. They were elated when the Episcopal Conference approved the proposal on April 27, 1911. A papal endorsement followed on June 29, the feast of Sts. Peter and Paul and henceforth the foundation day of the Catholic Foreign Mission Society of America.

With the papal approbation in hand, Walsh and Price chose a temporary site for the new seminary at Hawthorne, New York, and they began to transfer the files of *The Field Afar* magazine to the new location. The actual launching of the seminary came with a speed that surprised everyone, in great part due to the helping hands of three other women who had volunteered their services to the foreign mission project—Mary Louise Wholean,[20] Sara Sullivan, and Mary Dwyer. When Walsh notified the women to come to Hawthorne on January 6, 1912,[21] his secretary, Nora Shea, who also yearned to commit herself to the project, could not come with them. Her services were required in the Boston office until late summer. More significant, Mollie was not free to come at all because of a financial crisis in the family. Although she had been collaborating with Walsh since 1907, she was now needed at home for an unspecified time. Although obliged to disengage temporarily from the mission project, she remained as actively involved as she could. With Nora Shea, she visited Hawthorne twice in the ensuing months.

Those who assembled in Hawthorne found poor accommodations, a steady flow of work, and an uncertain future. Walsh had told them as much, underscoring that, after all, this was a journey of faith for all of them. The sense of uncertainty was intensified when, as early as March 19, 1912, Mary Louise Wholean felt a peculiar pain in her side. Surgery on April 1 confirmed that she had cancer and that she might have only six or seven years to live. Although offered the option to return home, she chose to stay with the group and to contribute her services for as long as she could.[22] Succeeding surgeries and treatments enabled her to participate actively in the life and work of Maryknoll up to within two months of her death in 1917.

When Mollie visited Hawthorne during the school holiday in February 1912, the women met her for the first time. Although they knew of her commitment to this foreign mission work from its inception, they now observed her willingness and ability to do any job that was needed. Her poise and self-assurance gave them a clearer sense of purpose and unity, characteristics that were also obvious to Father Walsh. If the group was to become a religious community—and he had written about that intention in *The Field Afar* as early as December 1911— one among them would have to assume the leadership. For this, Walsh clearly pinned his hopes on Mollie. From the beginning of their friendship in December 1906, Walsh had recognized Mollie's intelligence, her creativity, her generosity, and her high ideals. He had shared with her his knowledge of the church's foreign missions, encouraged her in her spiritual journey, and relied on her as his "co-worker."[23] He must have prayed that she would join them soon in Hawthorne, and permanently.

Another person who constantly brought joy into the stressful lives of the women was Mother Alphonsa Lathrop, OP. Born Rose Hawthorne, she was the third child of Nathaniel Hawthorne, the distinguished American novelist and short-story writer. With a keen sense of the social challenges of the new century, Mother Alphonsa had founded a community of Dominican Sisters in Hawthorne dedicated to the care of poor people who suffered from terminal cancer. This gentlewoman took a lively interest in the little community of "secretaries" who readily doubled as cooks and clerks, filling needs as they arose. Mother Alphonsa made their well-being her concern, especially when food and water were in short supply.

Inadvertently, it was Mother Alphonsa who would soon set the process in motion for Mollie's permanent return to Hawthorne. In July 1912, when Mollie came for a visit with Nora Shea, the two of them walked over to meet Mother Alphonsa. From that first encounter until Mother Alphonsa's death on July 9, 1926, she and Mollie were close friends, despite the disparity in their ages. Mollie was not yet thirty and Mother Alphonsa was sixty-one when they met.

Even before the two came to know each other well, Mollie's natural leadership was evident to Mother Alphonsa. At their first meeting in 1912 she urged Mollie to stay with the group, so much did she want to see the women's work succeed. Mollie explained her circumstances and, half in jest, told Mother Alphonsa that if someone gave her two thousand dollars she would be able to stay.[24] A few days later Mother Alphonsa channeled that exact sum to Mollie through Father Walsh. Appended was a note urging Mollie to use this gift to meet her obligations at home so that she could return to Hawthorne in the fall. Seventeen years later, in a talk to the community on January 6, 1929, Mother Mary Joseph mused, "I have always felt that, if that particular incident had not come up, the work of our particular branch would not have gone on that year, and I am sure that, if the Community had broken up then, another beginning would never have been made."[25]

Before returning to Boston to make the necessary arrangements and to take leave of her family, Mollie conspired with Father Walsh to purchase a property for Maryknoll's permanent home in Ossining, New York.[26] In order to avert any possible prejudice toward a priest buyer, Mollie Rogers would pose as a young woman buyer. Her chauffeur would be none other than James A. Walsh, well disguised in linen duster and goggles. The sale was finalized within three hours in the afternoon of August 17, 1912.[27] Three days later Mollie legally transferred "her" property to The Catholic Foreign Mission Society of America for one dollar.

Toward the end of August, Mollie wrote Mother Alphonsa from Boston to express her gratitude for her large monetary gift and to inform her of what had transpired in the family upon her return. "My people have been most generous, even before they knew of the great gift, and after the first passionate outbreak, unselfishly gave me up."[28] She also admitted to the wrenching separation that lay ahead: "My heart is a ragged old thing these days."[29] Her inner turmoil notwithstanding, when she looked back Mollie must have been amazed at how seriously God had taken her offer that June day in 1904 when she knelt in St. Mary's before the Blessed Sacrament. With what seemed hardly any effort on her part, God had guided her through unexpected obstacles into the foreign mission enterprise that was becoming her life.

Mollie returned to Hawthorne on September 9, accompanied by seventeen-year-old Margaret Shea, the sixth "secretary" and by far the youngest in the group. Margaret had been looking for a religious order. Until she found one that appealed to her, her confessor had suggested she volunteer to work in Father Walsh's foreign mission project. Mollie encouraged the younger woman: "Let's just go together and see what God has in store for us."[30] Margaret came with Mollie and never turned back.

A few days after Mollie and Margaret arrived in Hawthorne, Father Walsh acted on his intention to place Mollie in charge. After putting the matter to the group to ascertain its agreement,[31] on September 15 he named her "head of the household" until the feast of Epiphany, 1913.[32] Though the reason is not clear, he also bestowed on her the more formal name of Mary Joseph.[33] Although Mollie was only approaching her thirtieth birthday on October 27, she assumed her role as leader with grace.[34] She never distanced herself from the group, whether she spoke with them about the spiritual life, restraint, punctuality, or a change in schedule. She maintained that a dignified spirit was required at all times, especially in view of the growing mixed population at Maryknoll. The first six seminarians had arrived in mid-September.

Almost immediately, the task of all concerned was to move to Maryknoll, the recently acquired farm on Sunset Hill in Ossining, New York. Walsh had used the name Maryknoll on his stationery since his arrival at Hawthorne. In the 1912 October/November issue of *The Field Afar* he announced the new site and bestowed on it the permanent name of Maryknoll.

In his report to Rome at the end of the first year, Walsh discreetly described his growing missionary community:

> Towards the end of September we opened with six students, two for Theology and four for Philosophy. We have also with us three aspirant Brothers, and, in a private house at one corner of our grounds, and shortly to be enclosed, is a group of eight[35] faithful women, who are serving the cause by clerical and domestic assistance. Four of these have been aiding the work from the beginning. They are lay-women who would gladly welcome the religious life, and who are practically leading such, as is evidenced by their daily Communion, rule of silence, and willingness to give their labor to the Church without any material compensation.[36]

Thus, from the beginning of Maryknoll there existed three branches—the priests, the brothers, and the women who longed to be religious. Each branch came from the same tree, and each depended upon the others for its growth and mutual support. All shared the same founders with their ideals, aspirations, and spiritual motivation, growing together as one family with a common history and identity.

2

From "Secretaries"
to Women Religious

The November 1913 issue of *The Field Afar* contained a two-page article entitled "The Teresians of Maryknoll," referring to Teresa of Avila, the model Father Walsh had held up to the secretaries.[1] Walsh wanted his readers to know that they were a flourishing group on whose services the Society depended for its own development. They had increased from three to seven by the end of the year. In 1920, forty-two women would welcome the news announced in the March issue of *The Field Afar*[2] that "the Teresians" had been approved by Rome as a religious congregation. How did the women go from being "dedicated Teresians" in 1913 to being vowed religious in 1921? The span of eight years hints at a lengthy process that became mystifyingly cumbersome over the course of time. Rome's approval would be granted only after three petitions had been formally submitted.

The women's path toward religious life was a journey in faith from the outset, as noted by Walsh in the April 1920 issue of *The Field Afar*: "The little group of women at Hawthorne was an experiment, and, for each and all, it was an unusual sacrifice, because no assurance could be given to them that they would be anything more than laywomen, united by a common purpose and supported by their combined meagre salaries."[3]

The first three women met for the first time on January 1, 1912, at the Cenacle in New York, where they made a short retreat together prior to traveling to Hawthorne. Mary Louise Wholean's first entry in the *Teresian Diary* memorialized her sense of the mystery of God's hand in the project: "We were strangers to each other and differed in age, training and disposition, but we had been brought together and were henceforth to be united by the common desire of serving the cause of the foreign missions."[4]

The question of the women's future as a religious community was a regular topic of discussion, as noted in the *Teresian Diary*. Mary Louise Wholean's entry on June 5, 1912 mentions that Father Walsh had spoken about it with her that morning.[5] Religious life was uncharted territory for the women. Few, if any of them, had known religious Sisters or had ever had any opportunity to observe them firsthand. For this reason they relied heavily on Walsh for direction and assistance, and they were not disappointed. Almost as soon as the women arrived, Walsh suggested a daily timetable that would ensure the primacy of prayer in their busy lives. He also gave frequent conferences to nourish them spiritually. However, he regretted that he could do little, especially in the first year, to assist them in organizing their new community. As Mary Louise noted, it "would mean double work for him, and his work is already more than double what it ought to be."[6] However, the future of the secretaries remained uppermost among the many concerns that absorbed his energies. In time, Walsh would approach other congregations to assist the Teresians in their religious formation. From 1916 to 1920 he persistently sought to obtain canonical recognition from the Vatican on their behalf.

The Teresians marked their first anniversary at Maryknoll in January of 1913 with a retreat led by Father Henry Borgmann, a Redemptorist priest. They entered into this graced time with a clear ongoing desire for the vowed life. Mary Louise Wholean wrote that it seemed unfeasible simply to continue as they were, "on account of the necessity that we might feel of providing for the future."[7] The women felt there might not be a future at all unless they formed a permanent organization.[8] Accordingly, Father Borgmann led the group to a more profound understanding of the spirituality that would sustain them throughout this period. He spoke of Teresa of Avila, the model and patron Father Walsh had given them, emphasizing her thorough and down-to-earth approach to God. He further challenged the women with his favorite maxim, "Know thyself, know God." Mary Joseph, for whom the retreat was her first such experience, was totally caught up in the conferences and prayers. She was not alone. While the women had to continue with some of their work during the retreat, each one savored the time for reflection that strengthened their resolve to dedicate their lives to the work of foreign mission.

In the course of 1913 it was still not obvious just how the secretaries would go about becoming a religious congregation. Walsh realized that at the very least they would need the authorization of a bishop as well as initial formation in religious life. For this, he favored the Franciscan Missionaries of Mary, whom he had seen at work in the mission field and had greatly admired their spirit. Plans for their coming were initiated, but a critical letter went astray before arrangements could be finalized.[9] Walsh approached six other religious communities before receiving a favorable reply from the Sisters Servants of the Immaculate Heart of Mary in Scranton, Pennsylvania.

Two specific concerns had guided the search for a community that would provide formation in religious life. The first priority was for a congregation oriented to foreign mission and thereby adapted to that purpose. The second was for an American-based rather than European-based congregation in order to minimize the disparity between cultures.[10] Although the first priority was not met, the ideal perdured in the minds and hearts of the women. In those early days, as they became more familiar with conditions in mission lands, they envisioned becoming the kind of religious community that could readily adapt to the needs of the people. In the years that followed Mother Mary Joseph treated the exigencies for this expression of religious life at length in her conferences to the community under what she called the Maryknoll spirit.

Three Sisters of the Immaculate Heart of Mary were due to arrive at Maryknoll on September 15, 1914. Meanwhile, in early summer, Miss Julia Ward,[11] a benefactor of Maryknoll and a great friend of the Teresians, thought that Mary Joseph would be an ideal companion on her annual trip to Lourdes, France. She proposed her idea to Walsh, who agreed that a trip to Europe would assuredly broaden Mary Joseph's vision of the Catholic tradition. Mary Joseph herself felt this would be an awkward time to be away because the Immaculate Heart Sisters were soon to arrive at Maryknoll. Out of courtesy, she brought the matter to the superior, Mother Germaine, who also saw it as an opportunity that would benefit the entire group. Mary Joseph's experiences, especially in Rome, would indeed mark the development of the congregation in very significant ways.

Mary Joseph and Julia Ward sailed for France on July 15, 1914, in the face of impending war. They arrived in Lourdes on July 28, the very day war was declared. In retrospect, it seems strange that their travel plans would not have been scrapped in view of the volatile situation in Europe. To people in the United States, however, the situation did not appear that critical. There had been at least a half-dozen other conflicts in Europe in the previous decade. Americans assumed this one would also resolve itself and life would go on as usual.[12] Thus, even with the mobilization of troops all around them, Mary Joseph was focused on the daily stream of sick and disabled people being brought to the grotto at Lourdes. She was inspired by the tenderness with which the nurses and aides ministered to them.

The two pilgrims arrived in Rome just before Pius X's death on August 20, 1914, and they joined the throng of mourners in St. Peter's Basilica. Two weeks later, on September 3, Mary Joseph and Julia Ward were again among the faithful in St. Peter's Square to witness the white smoke that signaled the election of Benedict XV.

During the time Mary Joseph and Julia were in Rome—they were stranded there for an extra month because of the war—they visited historical sites, two of which were to leave a deep and lasting impression on Mary Joseph: the Church of San Stefano and the English hospital conducted by the Sisters of the Company of Mary, popularly known as the Blue Nuns. At San Stefano she learned anew what being a follower of Christ entailed. Thirty-four years later, in a talk to the Sisters, she vividly recalled the sobering display of various forms of martyrdom on the walls of the church: "[It] gave me an understanding that I had never had before of what one must endure for Christ if one is to be a true disciple of Christ." She cautioned them:

> It is all very well to talk and dream about the martyrdom that we would undergo. . . . However, we prepare ourselves for martyrdom in quite a different way—namely in the violence that we do to ourselves to keep our rule, as well as to do the little tasks that we don't like to do, and to do them in a spirit of faith, out of love of God. It is in that way that we build up the strength of character and the strength of purpose which would enable us, if the moment came, to endure and suffer martyrdom.[13]

The visit to this church taught her irrevocably that greatness or holiness was not limited to the extraordinary. The total gift of oneself applied as well, if not more so, to the mundane. No opportunity was to be overlooked.

Just as intuitively as Mary Joseph grasped the taproot of true holiness, she also understood that only a person nourished consistently on prayer could respond generously to divine love. This insight was confirmed by her observations in the hospital chapel of the Company of Mary. While some Sisters were out working with the poor and the sick, others kept a continual presence in prayer. Patterned on this example, perpetual adoration at the Maryknoll Sisters' chapel was initiated early in the congregation's history.[14] Prayer for one another would underscore the deep bond of faith among all Maryknollers. Years later Mother Mary Joseph also credited the Company of Mary for the idea of the Maryknoll Sisters Cloister, a group set apart to pray for the missions. Mother Mary Joseph hoped that both of these experiences, the total gift of oneself through martyrdom and the absolute need for a consistent life of prayer, would mark the congregation's character as it grew and developed.

Mary Joseph returned from her European pilgrimage on October 2, 1914, and quickly rejoined the group of Teresians who were two weeks into their novitiate formation. She found that the Teresians were disconcerted by the traditional convent practices they were learning. However awkward some of these may have seemed to her as well, they did not inhibit her spontaneity. Even as a novice she repeatedly demonstrated her genius for maintaining a balance between the demands of religious observance and the urgent work at hand. It was not long before the Immaculate Heart Sisters "began to hope for the end of *The Field Afar*,"[15] which, it seemed to them, was unduly distracting the novices. Mary Joseph and all the Teresians realized that the Immaculate Heart Sisters could not have known beforehand that the mailing of *The Field Afar* was a task that consumed a substantial number of days every month.[16] As Mary Joseph had done years before within the Rogers family, here again she deftly drew on her talent to offset potential conflicts by helping the IHMs understand how vital this mailing was for the life and continuation of the Foreign Mission Society.

After a year and a half of novitiate formation, on March 7, 1916, Father John T. McNicholas, OP, a close friend of Father Walsh, enrolled the Teresians as Dominican tertiaries. Beforehand, the Teresians had undergone a consultation process to consider groups with which they might affiliate. The Carmelites were attractive because of their intense life of prayer. Yet, the mission spirit of the Franciscans continued to appeal. Ultimately, however, the Dominican ideal of contemplation and action was deemed most suited to the apostolic life the Teresians envisioned for themselves,[17] and they looked forward to becoming a Dominican congregation in the near future.

Before the ceremony, however, Father McNicholas spoke of a recent ecclesiastical decree that specified that permission to found a new religious congregation had to come from Rome. No longer could a local bishop or cardinal approve the foundation of a new community of religious such as the Teresians. The women had expected that their community would be officially established at the end of their novitiate formation. Now they learned that their novitiate was not even valid.[18] Although deeply disappointed, the Teresians did not lose heart, except for Mary Dwyer, who had become impatient for more stability in her life. In April 1916, she withdrew from the Maryknoll project and returned to Boston. The Sisters of the Immaculate Heart of Mary could have returned to Scranton immediately, but they chose to remain with the Teresians until the completion of their agreement on July 1, 1916.[19] Their departure was softened by a concession Walsh had obtained from Cardinal John Farley of New York. While the latter usually insisted on two full unbroken years of novitiate, in the case of the Teresians he agreed that once the permission was obtained, only one canonical year would be required.[20]

By July 1916, seventeen Teresians were determined to be recognized as a bona fide religious congregation. Their first petition to Rome in the previous month had succumbed to Vatican bureaucracy and was returned undelivered because it had been sent to the wrong office. Although mailed again immediately, the women waited six months for an answer, only to be advised that they could organize as a society of pious women without vows. This did not include permission to begin a valid novitiate.[21] Still undaunted, there was much the Dominican tertiaries could do to advance their plans. Through the mediation of Father McNicholas, OP, the Dominican Sisters of Sinsinawa, Wisconsin, sent Sister Ruth Devlin, OP, to teach Dominican spirituality, prayer, and customs and to assist in the formulation of the proposed constitutions for the new congregation. Even though she was with the Teresians only from April to August 1916, she was instrumental in helping them lay a solid foundation for the future congregation.

Just when the Teresians were gathering momentum to realize their dream, Mary Louise Wholean became bedridden. Nothing more could be done for her cancer. Her mother came to Maryknoll to nurse her by day, and Mary Joseph stepped in as night nurse until Mary Louise died on February 19, 1917, at age thirty-five. She was the first Maryknoller to pass into eternity. From the beginnings at Hawthorne, January 6, 1912, Mary Louise had been the faithful and gifted chronicler—author of the *Teresian Diary*—until December 21, 1916, when she made her last entry. James Anthony Walsh's eulogy spoke eloquently of the incalculable loss her death meant for all of Maryknoll.[22] He praised her "fine, well-trained mind," her keen intellect, and good judgment "unbiased by sentiment." Mary Louise had "a heart of gold, affectionate and loyal." Most especially, Walsh extolled her faith as "the fruit of prayerful searching for the truth, and fidelity to each succeeding grace that God dropped into her soul."

Walsh had first met Mary Louise after speaking on behalf of the Society for the Propagation of the Faith in a little church in South Natick, Massachusetts, near Wellesley College. She was one of two women from the college who had attended and spoken to him about "the strong and lively interest in foreign missions taken by their non-Catholic classmates," and how they wanted to kindle a similar interest among the Catholic students. There was no further contact between Walsh and the women until seven years later, when Mary Louise suddenly called Walsh for an appointment. He and Price had just returned from Rome with the pope's blessing to start the seminary. Walsh recalled Mary Louise's first words: "I don't know why I have come, or what I can do; but something has been urging me for several years to give my life-work to the interests of foreign missions." As they talked together Walsh learned that she had never heard of *The Field Afar* magazine and knew nothing at all about the newly projected Catholic Foreign Mission Society of America. He concluded, "God had chosen her . . . and she had responded."[23]

As winter turned into spring it became obvious that the care and death of Mary Louise had taken a toll on Mary Joseph. She, whose health and stamina had always been amazing, began to experience illnesses that would continue during the rest of her life.[24] That very spring, as war with Germany loomed, she had surgery from which she would need several months to recuperate. In all that time, if Mary Joseph had any fears or self-doubts about the women's status as a group, no one would have suspected it. Although she felt unequal to the task of preparing the group for religious life—since she knew so little about it herself—she tried to maintain a single-hearted joy and enthusiasm for the mission that had brought them together in the first place.[25]

The combination of events—Mary Louise's death, the war, and Mary Joseph's illness—cast a deep shadow over the life of the Teresians, but as women of faith, they pressed forward. The second petition was sent to Rome sometime in August 1917. It was answered six months later by a second refusal in a letter dated February 2, 1918. Years later, on February 14, 1940, in a talk to the community, Mother Mary Joseph elaborated on this second refusal. She spoke of how Rome insisted the Teresians give clearer definition to the scope of their work and means of support.[26]

But there was another unspoken reason that they learned of subsequently from Father McNicholas. In Rome, the cardinal concerned with their process had no confidence that American women were courageous enough or strong enough to withstand the rigors of mission life. He thought of them as soft and so accustomed to luxury that any idea they might have of serving in mission was doomed to failure. Mother Mary Joseph quipped, "We always thought it was fortunate that that Cardinal died."[27] She went on to explain that he was succeeded by his own brother, who had personally witnessed the valor of American women in war zones. It was what had led him to decide in favor of the Teresians in 1920.

However, back in 1918, they still had to deal with the second refusal. Rome was stipulating further that since they desired to be a congregation dedicated to the work of foreign missions, they would need to be open to working with other mission societies besides Maryknoll. Mary Joseph, who had always perceived the identity and role of the Teresians as an integral part of the Maryknoll family, had never imagined working apart from the Maryknoll Society. The letter from Rome further required that the Sisters develop autonomous structures of government and be financially independent from the Society.

Mary Joseph needed some time to mull over the implications of these demands. Shrewdly, she perceived that the changes could effect a distancing between the Sisters and the Society. A difficult meeting with Father Walsh over these issues ensued. She was for holding off, because, as she wrote Walsh later that day, "it didn't seem right or true to me; even if it was only to get permission to start, it would stand as an expression of our desires."[28] In the same note she implicitly accepted the wisdom in the letter from Rome when she acknowledged, "It is evident that we must be independent and leave you free." But she hastened to affirm, "Measure our love for the Society by your own." From the beginning, Mary Joseph and the Teresians had given their lives for the whole of Maryknoll, and she was determined to uphold that integrity.

By the end of 1918 there were twenty-five Teresians who worked and prayed and longed to be foreign missioners. In September they had participated in the first departure ceremony of four Maryknoll priests for China, and there were already openings for mission awaiting the Teresians in Seattle, Los Angeles, and Yeungkong, China. More women were coming, and still they had no permission to begin a novitiate. Walsh wrote many letters to those who might have influence, including an urgent plea in March 1919 to his good friend John McNicholas, now bishop of Duluth, Minnesota. McNicholas immediately prepared a third petition, which was hand carried to Rome on June 7, 1919.[29]

A favorable response to the third petition was anticipated, and once again McNicholas contacted the Sinsinawa Dominicans. The Maryknoll women had received their initial introduction to Dominican religious life from Sister Ruth Devlin, OP. Now, they would continue a more intentional formation in the Dominican tradition with Sister Fidelia Delaney, OP, whom Mary Joseph described as "a sister of ripe experience, having been a religious forty-three years."[30] So quick was she to capture the spirit and purpose of Maryknoll that Father Walsh dubbed her "Maryknoll's grandmother."

Within two months of Sister Fidelia's arrival from Sinsinawa, news reached Father Walsh at Maryknoll that Father Thomas Frederick

Price, stricken with acute appendicitis, had died in Hong Kong on September 12, 1919, only a year after his arrival in China. He was fifty-nine years old, the second Maryknoller to die. As a dedicated priest in North Carolina for many years and co-founder of the Maryknoll Society, he was known and respected by many church leaders and Catholic laity. Years later, Walsh would recall his "associate of sweet memory," reiterating his personal conviction that in the beginnings of Maryknoll, more was owed to Price than to himself.[31]

Sister Fidelia's work was to begin in earnest when the Teresians received the joyful news on February 14, 1920, that they could now be established officially as a diocesan religious institute.[32] The date of the document became the canonical foundation day of the Foreign Mission Sisters of St. Dominic—the new official title for the Teresians of Maryknoll.[33]

The formal novitiate opened immediately. On July 2, 1920, the community received a letter from Father Louis Theissling, master general of the Order of Friars Preachers, warmly welcoming them into the Dominican family.[34] Also, in July's issue of *The Field Afar*, Walsh published a letter he had received from James E. Walsh in China: "The sisters can begin to plan their work on the missions [of Yeungkong, Kochow and Loting] . . . orphanage, girls' schools, and medical dispensaries."[35] With such promise, the final year of novitiate assumed unprecedented purpose.

In 1944, reflecting with the community on the women's direction toward religious life, Mother Mary Joseph was convinced that

> even if this grace had been denied us [recognition by Rome], those of us here at the time would have persevered as long as there was any need of our service, because we had given ourselves up completely to the work for foreign missions. But I am equally sure that few would have joined us—equally sure that our members would not have increased. Not that girls were less generous than we were, but naturally, directors of souls, confessors, parents of girls were unwilling to have them give up a life of certainty to go into a work in which there was no guarantee of stability.[36]

Mary Joseph and the Teresians knew from the start that religious life would provide them with the stability they needed. Instinctively, they also perceived that to sustain the call to foreign mission, their style of religious life would need to be readily adaptable to local needs. As they laid the foundation for the future, the women's faithful perseverance and foresight ensured their place, and that of all who would follow, in the world of mission.

3

The Field Afar

Foreign mission rose as a permanent beacon on the women's horizon during the founding decade. Visiting missionaries from Asia made the lure of China compelling. Though the women knew not how it would come about, they believed that someday, like their Maryknoll brothers, they too would sail to fields afar.

Typically, the women did not wait for everything to be in place before taking their first steps in mission. In February 1920, the same month that the Sisters were canonically established as a foreign mission congregation, Mary Joseph acted on two invitations for Sisters to work among Japanese immigrants on the West Coast of the United States. She conferred with Archbishop Hayes of New York, asking for his approval and blessing so that four Sisters, who were willing to delay their novitiate year and first vows, could proceed to mission in Los Angeles and Seattle. Among them was Margaret Shea, now Sister Gemma, who had come to Hawthorne with Mollie on September 9, 1912, and whom Mollie had encouraged to come and see what God had in store for them.

While the first Maryknoll Sisters' missions were being established on the West Coast, twenty-one Sisters at Maryknoll, including Mary Joseph, completed their novitiate. After they professed their vows on February 15, 1921, Mary Joseph was appointed first prioress by Archbishop Hayes and was henceforth to be called Mother Mary Joseph. Almost immediately, the archbishop permitted those Sisters who had been assigned to mission on the West Coast and who had not participated in the novitiate year also to make their vows. Arrangements were made for them to do so in their places of mission the following month.

A second group of novices at Maryknoll made their vows in August of that same year, bringing the total of professed Sisters to thirty-eight. The steady increase had convinced both Father Walsh and Mother Mary Joseph that it was time to assign the first group of Sisters to China. Mother Mary Joseph announced the mission assignments on

June 29, with the first departure ceremony taking place on September 12. Two weeks later, six Sisters were on their way to China.

The 1921 summer issues of *The Field Afar* carefully tracked the Maryknoll personnel, including their movement to and in China: "After ten years, [Maryknoll] reckons the number of its family . . . at 329, divided as follows: Priests, 35; Auxiliary Brothers, 22; Major Seminary Students, 92; Preparatory College Students, 78; Sisters, 102."[1] By year's end the total number of Maryknoll personnel in China would reach twenty-four.

There was a great need in China for missionaries like these young professed Sisters. Walsh's editorials in *The Field Afar* consistently called for young men and women who were willing to leave their families and nation for the sake of God's reign in this world. The growing response indicated that his missionary call was reaching many hearts, and Maryknoll flourished, even when missionary service was still a very new idea for Catholics in the United States. In 1923, the Maryknoll Society sent forth its sixth group of men and the Sisters' Congregation its third group, to work hand in hand with the Fathers and Brothers. At the end of 1923, Maryknollers in South China numbered forty-six, eighteen of whom were Sisters.

The pioneer Maryknoll Missioners who arrived in China in 1918 and the years immediately following had little preparation in Chinese culture, language, history, or politics. During their formation at Maryknoll, which took place during the years of World War I (1914–18), they had been exposed to China's ferment through the perceptions of foreign missionaries and as recounted in *The Field Afar*. Thus Maryknollers left for mission in China with a very limited understanding of the volatile socio-political context into which they would be immersed. The scope of the brewing storms and the convulsive changes that were to engulf the land were beyond the range of their experience or imagination.

The fall of the Manchu Dynasty and the birth of the Chinese Republic/Republic of China in 1911 under Sun Yat-sen had hastened the rise of warlords, who vied for power. The constant conflicts gave rise to banditry that severely disrupted China's social fabric and greatly complicated missionary activity. As foreign nationals, missionaries were relatively safe. By contrast, the Chinese people often suffered injury—even death—at the hands of the bandits.

When Sun Yat-sen died in 1925, subversive Marxist groups were already forming in both the north and the south of China. One group was attached to Sun Yat-sen's southern political party, the Kuomintang (KMT), while the other was composed of a group of intellectuals at the

University of Peking in the north. In the south, Chou-en-Lai, head of the political department of the KMT's military academy, indoctrinated the cadets in Marxist ideology. In the north, Mao Tse-tung, a former student and librarian at the University of Peking, agitated for the organization of China's laborers into a Communist Party. In addition, Japan also had its eyes on China. To Western observers, Japan's domination of Korea and Formosa (Taiwan) and its incursions into Manchuria made its eventual conquest of China appear inevitable.

In 1926, Chinese patriots led by Chiang Kai-shek under the banner of the KMT mounted a major military campaign to reunify the country. When Chiang Kai-shek reached Shanghai in the spring of 1927, Mao's workers, who were already in control of the city, readily gave it over to the military commander. A few weeks later Chiang Kai-shek abruptly disarmed the workers and brutally purged the Communists from the Nationalist Party.[2] The Communists went underground and into the countryside, to emerge later as one of two major forces that threatened both the Nationalist regime and the missionaries. The other major force, as noted above, was Japan. In 1931, the Japanese began their large-scale military intervention in China by seizing Manchuria, severely restricting the movement of missionaries.[3] At the same time, the Communists focused on organizing the peasantry and establishing themselves firmly among them. After World War II they would sweep the country.

The China to which Maryknoll Sisters were assigned in 1923 was in grave inner turmoil. Despite this turmoil Mother Mary Joseph understood that having firsthand exposure and knowledge of mission conditions were essential for her leadership of the community. She also wanted to experience the Sisters' life for herself. Heedless of the hardships she would almost certainly encounter during China's heyday of banditry, she was determined to accompany the third group of Sisters departing for China.

The group that sailed from Seattle with Mother Mary Joseph on September 23, 1923, included eleven Maryknollers: seven Sisters, three priests, and one auxiliary Brother. At the first port of call in Yokohama, their initial view of Asia left them speechless. They stood aghast at the unspeakable destruction from an earthquake that had struck Japan only a month earlier. In Tokyo and Yokohama alone it was estimated that ninety thousand people had died.

At the next Japanese port of Kobe, a city not affected by the devastating quake, the missionaries were taken aback once again, this time by the emaciated condition of their fellow missioner, Father Patrick Byrne, Maryknoll's first missioner in Korea. Father Byrne had traveled from Shingishu to welcome his brother and sister Maryknollers to Asia. Mother Mary Joseph was shocked at Byrne's appearance. He admitted that he had been sick with severe dysentery for several weeks and was eating very little. Her suggestion that he go with them to Shanghai for medical care met with no resistance.[4] Unabashedly and lovingly, Mother Mary Joseph carried the responsibilities that genuinely belonged to her role as one of the three founders of the Maryknoll Movement.

The arrival of the ship in Shanghai was a moving event for the missioners. They would soon be heading for their various destinations in China. During this brief stop the missioners visited charitable works that Sisters would help to staff some years later.[5] The next scheduled stop was Kowloon, Hong Kong, on October 15, 1923. Sister Mary Paul McKenna, the superior of the Maryknoll Sisters in both Hong Kong and Yeungkong, joined Mother Mary Joseph at this point of her visitation. Together, they met with various missionary societies and learned about their works, organizations, and the people they served.

Throughout this journey Mother Mary Joseph carefully pondered every experience from the prevailing lawlessness she encountered in the Chinese villages to the vagaries of travel in China. The following entry in her *Diary* describes with gracious good humor a typical excursion on a Chinese junk in the early years of the twentieth century. With Father Francis X. Ford, who had been in the first group assigned to China and who now accompanied and guided them on their journey, the travelers were en route for Yeungkong, where Maryknoll Sisters were already in mission.

> We couldn't stand up, so we squatted as best we could and ate our supper. Then we tried to settle ourselves. . . . We could not even sit up straight on our shelf we were so close to the beams. . . . The place was infested with rats, enormous spiders, and cockroaches, and the night was punctured by cries of distress when unwelcome visitors explored ears and faces. We said night prayers and sang every song we could recall—sacred and profane—and I believe we all got forty winks before morning. . . . How good it was to get up to the deck and breathe pure air again! We had a fine day on deck although the sun was very hot and we were badly burned in spite of our umbrellas.[6]

There followed another full night and another full day before the junk anchored at Yeungkong. And this was only the beginning.

This first visitation would be a journey of more than seven months, in the course of which Mother Mary Joseph sometimes found herself in the midst of a raid by bandits. In November 1923, just as she and Father Ford were about to begin their journey back to Hong Kong, bandits invaded Yeungkong. She witnessed streams of people flocking into the mission compound, desperate to escape the marauding gangs. In such instances she would simply settle down and help out where she could. As the bandits sacked the city and hundreds of men, women, and children huddled inside the walls of the compound, Mother Mary Joseph welcomed them with her few words of greeting and her smile.[7] She aptly epitomized one of the attendant effects of this violence in her *Diary*: "At present it is very difficult to make the progress one would wish, for no sooner is a thing well started than the bandits or soldiers come and everything has to be suspended for a time."[8]

What she witnessed, in fact, was to be the oft-repeated experience of many missioners over the years and in different countries, that of seeing their work suspended and, more often than not, totally destroyed.

Mother Mary Joseph's last stop, in February 1924, was at Father Patrick Byrne's mission in Shingishu, Korea. There, she and Sister Mary Paul McKenna had arranged to make their final vows as Maryknoll Sisters. On February 11 the two of them "knelt on the floor [during Father Byrne's Mass] with the women and the children many of whom received Communion with us and for us." To Mother Mary Joseph, the moment of their vows was "so tense, so full of meaning . . . in that little Korean chapel. There was nothing to distract us—and everything to remind us of our obligations: poverty—chastity—obedience—foreign missions—sacrifice—restraint—souls."[9]

The stories, letters, and diaries of Mother Mary Joseph's first mission visitation to Asia in 1923 and 1924 reflect her growth in apostolic leadership, compassion, and faith. Her narratives and the stories told by those with whom she traveled inspired whole new approaches to mission. Again and again she had experienced personally what mission life meant: "isolation, sacrifice, and joy only in proportion to the closeness of one's union with God and to the spiritual resources within one's self."[10]

In the July-August 1924 issue of *The Field Afar*, Father Francis X. Ford published an article in which he expounded on the tangible effects of her style as she visited the China missions: "Mother became one of the Chinese family, not a mere friend. She saw China from the inside of kitchens and interior of the family quarters. . . . The women guiding boats or doing coolie's work would chat with her unreservedly, fully confident that she could divine their thoughts."[11]

Reflecting on Mother Mary Joseph's visit, Ford began to imagine new ways to gain "a permanent foothold of the Church in our missions."[12] Earlier, in February 1924, he had written more personally to Walsh that Mother Mary Joseph's trip "emphasized the hold our Sisters will have on Chinese women and the utter need of such influence to gain these women's hearts."[13] With Mother Mary Joseph's approval and blessing, Ford sent the Sister-missioners "two by two," like the early apostles, to the most remote parts of his territory, first in Yeungkong and later in Kaying. He urged the Sisters to become experts as first contacts, leading the women to "Catholicism, instructing them for baptism, and watching over them during their first years as new Catholics." It was a method "without precedent in the mission history of the Catholic Church."[14]

Mother Mary Joseph arrived home at Maryknoll in April 1924 to a jubilant welcome. The women who had entered the community during her absence were elated to meet the one about whom they had heard so much. She, in turn, was eager to encourage them and all the Sisters in their mission vocation, especially in view of the reality that awaited them. They needed to know now that their vocation required a well-grounded spirituality and uncommon stamina.

4

A Community for Mission

Mother Mary Joseph reflected deeply on the apostolic challenges of China. From her first mission visitation in the early 1920s, she observed that the Sisters needed a much more thorough preparation for the reality they would encounter, especially in view of the exigencies of direct evangelization. For all the Sisters, without exception, she saw a firm grounding in theology and scripture, together with Chinese language and culture as paramount.

Shortly after Mother Mary Joseph's return, the community prepared to say goodbye to Sister Fidelia Delaney, who had completed five years at Maryknoll and was now returning to her own community, the Dominican Sisters of Sinsinawa. Sister Fidelia had formed the Maryknoll novices in religious life according to the Dominican ideal of contemplation and action. She had come as novice director and teacher and had resonated harmoniously with her novices as they journeyed toward foreign mission. Upon her death in 1943, Mother Mary Joseph eulogized her for the readers of *The Field Afar*:

> Sister Fidelia brought to her work a brilliant mind, lofty ideals, the charm of a warmly loving heart, a delightful fund of humor, an immense generosity, deep humility, wells of common sense, and a most attractive, vitalizing spirituality. . . . Under her prudent guidance . . . [y]ears which might easily have been cluttered with "spiritualities" and rendered barren were marked by unusual material and spiritual progress. Her name will ever be held in [our] grateful and prayerful remembrance.[1]

Sister Fidelia's departure signaled a new level of maturity for the Maryknoll Sisters. One of them, Sister Mary Lumena McMahon, took over the formation of the novices. The young community then began to prepare for the Congregation's first General Chapter to be held in May 1925.

Mother Mary Joseph had served as superior from the time of her arrival at Maryknoll in 1912. Her recent visitation of the Sisters in Asia and the West Coast of the United States had considerably broadened her understanding of missionary life and enhanced her leadership acumen in the eyes of the Sisters. When the day came for the delegates to elect the Sister who would serve the Congregation as mother general for a six-year term, Mother Mary Joseph, who was so revered in the community, was the uncontested choice and was thus the first elected mother general of the Maryknoll Sisters.[2]

Mother Mary Joseph was only a few months into her term of office in the fall of 1925 when the Newman Club chaplain of two New York City colleges invited her to address the students.[3] Her talk unwittingly propelled her into the limelight of the current discussion concerning Catholic education. She was introduced as a striking example of how it is possible for Catholics who attend non-Catholic colleges not only to keep the faith but also to practice the counsels of perfection. It was quite natural for Mother Mary Joseph to tell the story of how her mission vocation had emerged and been nurtured by the vibrant missionary activity of the Protestants during her years at Smith College. Her aim was to affirm the students in the practice of their faith and to convince them that Catholic students at secular universities could be both good Catholics and potential missioners.[4]

The news release that followed sparked the ire of the Jesuit editor of *America*. He strongly criticized Mother Mary Joseph's talk in his editorial of December 19, 1925. Maryknollers in Asia, Rome, and the United States, as well as many other friends, including Jesuits, quickly rallied to Mother Mary Joseph's support. From the readers of *America* she received a wide mixture "of advice, sympathy, censure, inquiry, lamentations, and hurrahs."[5] In her own response to the editor she agreed that young Catholics, especially those whose early religious training had been neglected, would be much better off in a Catholic college. "But," she added,

> since there are those who, either through necessity or choice, are in secular universities, does it not behoove us, who are keenly interested in every soul, to help keep warm their love of God and his Church? . . . My talk had only this intent, and it is truly painful and regrettable that my words have been taken from their setting and freighted with a meaning they never held. And who will undo the harm this criticism has done me, not personally, but in my position as Religious superior of a Congregation devoted to the spread of the

faith, a work in which obedience to the slightest wish of the Church must of necessity be law?[6]

The *America* publicity, which ceased within a few months, had several beneficial effects, one of which may have been to draw candidates to the Maryknoll Sisters. While young women had been coming to Maryknoll in groups of five or six, by the mid-1920s they were joining in thirties and forties. The "controversy" also ratified publicly Mother Mary Joseph's unequivocal appreciation of Catholic education. In addition, it established that within a decade and a half Maryknoll had become well known in the church in the United States and that Mother Mary Joseph herself was held in high esteem.[7]

As a result of the unprecedented increase in membership, Mother Mary Joseph faced two urgent concerns: the need to establish a firm financial base for ongoing support of the Sisters and to construct a building to provide sufficient accommodations for them. She began by initiating several small income-generating projects at Maryknoll and also obtained permission for the Sisters to solicit donations for their work at the doors of churches, initially in the dioceses of Philadelphia, St. Louis, and New York. Thus began the Maryknoll Sisters' appeals to American Catholics through their parishes. The Sisters were constantly amazed at the way the parish priests, Sisters, and parishioners welcomed them. They were received into convents, provided with lodging and meals, and ushered into parish schools to talk about missionary life and Maryknoll. During those early years Mother Mary Joseph also received much-needed assistance from several religious congregations that offered college scholarships for the Sisters.[8]

On September 1, 1929, ground was broken for the Motherhouse across the street from the Society seminary[9]—and the following month the stock market crashed. Hence, it was principally through prayer, and perhaps a genuine miracle, that the contract for construction was signed on May 1, 1930, and that the Sisters moved in on March 2, 1932.[10] While Mother Mary Joseph experienced joy and satisfaction in the clearer self-identity their own Motherhouse would give the Sisters, she was also concerned that this distancing from the Maryknoll priests and Brothers might cause the Sisters to forget all that had been given to them by the Society since the beginnings at Hawthorne in 1912.[11]

The devastating effects of the Great Depression tempered Mother Mary Joseph's sense of accomplishment. In a letter to Sister Fidelia, who remained a close friend, she described the months that followed the move to the Motherhouse as "extraordinarily difficult." "Unless help comes from some supernatural source, I do not know what we shall do, for our income is cut off almost entirely by the depression outside. Still God has sustained us in a most striking way through the years, and I cannot feel that anything untoward will happen now."[12]

The major development projects that Mother Mary Joseph undertook during her first term in office (1925–31) did not divert her attention from her most compelling purpose: the formation of a community for mission. Her first mission visitation in Asia in 1923 and 1924, and the second one in 1926 and 1927, contributed to her unique vision of the qualities needed for the Maryknoll Sisters, both personally and communally. Each Sister was called to develop her own individuality with her own particular gifts. Together, as the body of Christ, the Maryknoll Sisters were to form a strongly bonded community of apostolic women sent to give witness to God's reign throughout the world. Her mission visitations, which were extensive, had informed her about how demanding mission life could be. She had observed that no matter how great the efforts, the adequate preparation of Sisters could not keep pace with the rapid development of the Asian and Pacific missions. To this end she formulated a Mission Policy in 1929 that she sent for review and suggestions to Father Walsh and to the Society and Congregation superiors in Asia.[13]

With indomitable faith and courage Mother Mary Joseph began to prepare for the General Chapter of 1931. She had been thinking ahead to the Constitutions that would need to be written at this chapter; she wanted them to reflect the requisites of the missionary vocation. She and the Council carefully formulated the missionary phase of the Sisters' life and ministry, taking into consideration the suggestions that had come in from the review of the Mission Policy. They were bound by the constraints of a schema for Constitutions designed by the Congregation for Religious in Rome, yet they pressed on, convinced that the missionary vocation "demanded something different from the generally accepted religious manner."[14] It required "the sanctifying of one's natural qualities."[15] Incorporating innovative ideas in precise ecclesiastical language was a daunting albeit rewarding task. On the eve of the General Chapter, Mother Mary Joseph told the community at Maryknoll that once the draft had been thoroughly reviewed by the delegates, she was confident the community would have Constitutions they could claim as their very own.[16]

The delegates to the General Chapter of 1931 reelected Mother Mary Joseph for a second six-year term and then set themselves to work on the Constitutions. Among many other things, this chapter explicitly identified the priority of forming native sisterhoods, just as

Pope Benedict XV had enjoined the Maryknoll Society "to form at the earliest opportunity a native clergy as the most efficacious means of perpetuating its works of conversion."[17] The Sisters were as convinced as their Maryknoll Brothers of the need to build up the local church: "Maryknoll's overall purpose was to spread the Gospel among non-Christians, but a special emphasis was given to building an indigenous Church by training native priests, Sisters, and catechists, by stimulating the laity to apostolic activity and by founding Christian institutions."[18] Eventually, the Sisters initiated six indigenous novitiates among the twenty foreign mission centers established by Mother Mary Joseph and the Sisters in Asia during the 1930s.[19]

The most significant decision made at the 1931 General Chapter was the establishment of a cloistered branch of the Maryknoll Sisters' Congregation. The foundation of the cloister can be traced to the dream that had taken hold of Mary Joseph in 1914 when she and Julia Ward visited the Sisters of the Company of Mary in Rome.[20] Mary Joseph had noticed that the Sisters in ministry in that community were always accompanied by others in prayer. From that moment, Mother Mary Joseph yearned for a community of Sisters who would fulfill such a role at Maryknoll.

Over the years, several Sisters had expressed personal interest in a Maryknoll contemplative life such as she envisioned. Before the 1931 chapter, Mother Mary Joseph's consultations on the matter had met with both consternation and encouragement.[21] Some people adamantly maintained that a contemplative community simply could not exist alongside an active community. Having witnessed otherwise, Mother Mary Joseph and her council believed that God's hand was in this decision. On October 3, 1932, ten Maryknoll Sisters were formally enclosed in the old farmhouse on the hill overlooking the Motherhouse. During the previous week Mother Mary Joseph had given them a retreat in which she stressed that they would always remain an integral part of the Congregation yet be set apart as a community of life and prayer for the entire Maryknoll family and other missioners throughout the world.[22] She also affirmed that the prayer of the cloistered Sisters would be an ongoing reminder to all Maryknollers that in order to thrive as missioners, a personal "life of prayer was an essential touchstone."[23]

Not a full year had elapsed since the opening of the cloister when Mother Mary Joseph traveled to Rome to attend the ordination of James Anthony Walsh as titular bishop of Siene.[24] He was ordained on June 29, 1933, the twenty-second anniversary of the Maryknoll Society's foundation. By then, there were over nine hundred Maryknollers to rejoice in the honor that the church had bestowed on the Maryknoll founder.[25]

James Anthony Walsh, who was sixty-six years old when he became bishop, appeared to be healthy. Within the year, however, he needed to take time off for treatments, which everyone believed would restore his health.[26] Walsh spent the early months of 1935 in the warm climate of Jacksonville, Florida, at St. Vincent's Hospital. He returned to Maryknoll in April and resumed his role as father general. Although he was not well enough to participate in the administration of the Society, in June he ordained sixteen priests and presided at the departure ceremony.

That same month the news arrived from South China that Monsignor Francis X. Ford, vicar apostolic of Kaying Prefecture, had been named bishop. Ford had been the first student to arrive at Maryknoll in September 1912 and was in the first group of Maryknoll missioners to go to China in 1918. He specifically requested that his ordination be at Maryknoll and by his own father general, Bishop James Anthony Walsh. Walsh remained surprisingly well as he anticipated this privilege. Ford's ordination to the episcopacy on September 21, 1935, seemed to be a culmination and fulfillment of Walsh's life. It was also a magnificent moment for Mother Mary Joseph, as Bishop Ford looked to her as a spiritual mother.[27]

By mid-October 1935 Walsh's health had deteriorated noticeably. Mother Mary Joseph received a poignant note from him on her fifty-third birthday, October 27, thanking her for her "devoted loyal friendship": "You have been to me as a sister and my prayer in gratitude for the privilege is that God may give you abundant graces for the years of service that lie ahead for you."[28]

It was clear now that Bishop Walsh was dying of lung cancer. He lingered for several months, and Mother Mary Joseph often spent time quietly visiting with him. Just before Christmas, at his request, each of his Maryknoll sons and daughters filed by his bed and knelt to receive his final blessing. He died on April 14, 1936. Bishop Walsh had prepared a moving farewell message for each branch of the Maryknoll family. In part, these were his last formal words to the Sisters:

> Before leaving earth, let me acknowledge that I owe to your community no small portion of the success which has been credited to Maryknoll. Your generous and capable services and, above all, your constant prayers, have been with Maryknoll from the beginning. No one knows this better than I, and no one should be more grateful. . . . I leave with you the affection of a father for his daughters, my

one regret being that in these later years I could not know you individually as I would. It is a comforting thought that Mother Mary Joseph is being spared for your guidance and inspiration. May God keep her strong for many years to come.[29]

Within a month of Bishop Walsh's death, Mother Mary Joseph published a four-page article entitled "Out of the Years" in *The Field Afar* in appreciation of his life. She recalled the graced collaboration she had enjoyed with James A. Walsh in the foundation of Maryknoll:

I speak . . . of [nearly thirty] years of blessed friendship and privileged association with our Father General . . . From the beginning there were the substantial elements of this triple-branched family— the students, Maryknoll's future missioners; lay helpers, the future auxiliary Brotherhood; and the "Secretaries," Maryknoll's Sisters-to-be. We were closely bound by a common interest—the missions, by a strong spirit of mutual helpfulness and by a common father's affectionate protection.[30]

The death of Bishop Walsh was a deeply spiritual experience of pain and wonder, of aloneness and appreciation, of sorrow and joy, and of loss and hope for Mother Mary Joseph. The last of the three Maryknoll founders, she would live on for nearly twenty years, faithfully bearing witness to the spirit and charism of Maryknoll.

5

Last of the Founders

After the death of James Anthony Walsh, Mother Mary Joseph continued to lead the Sisters with the steadfastness of a founder. A new generation of leadership in the Catholic Foreign Mission Society of America took its place beside her. To succeed James Anthony Walsh as superior general, in 1936 the Society elected James Edward Walsh, who, in 1927, had been made bishop of the Kongmoon Vicariate at Sancian Island.[1] The younger Walsh had been in the first group assigned to China in 1918. He was also the first to write back in 1920 regarding mission openings for the Sisters, even before they were officially recognized as a religious congregation.

The immediate concern of Mother Mary Joseph in 1936 was preparation for the third General Chapter in July 1937. She invited Bishop James E. Walsh to give the opening talk and was deeply gratified by his message, which became the point of reference at this chapter. The bishop delivered a stirring commendation of the contribution of the Maryknoll Sisters in China from 1921 through 1937:

> Your vocation . . . consists in being missioners the same as the priests. . . . You do everything and anything connected with mission work, and you should consider yourselves apostles. You are a missionary congregation, and the emphasis with you would be in evangelical work, the same as in our own case. You are not merely a group of auxiliaries . . . doing what you are told. You brought something new—the Woman Apostolate.[2]

Bishop Walsh's understanding of the role of women in mission was remarkable for that era. Mother Mary Joseph responded to his words with manifest delight as she exclaimed to the delegates: "Never has anyone spoken to us in this way before."[3] She recounted for them some of the early history, noting that while James Anthony Walsh's appreciation of the women had been unquestionable, he had thought of them more as auxiliaries in the development of the Society. To some extent the women "auxiliaries" had shared his appraisal of their place in the foreign mission enterprise.[4] However, in the expansive atmosphere of Maryknoll, it was not surprising that the "auxiliaries" should begin to imagine themselves in foreign mission. Mother Mary Joseph continued, "As we developed and expressed more and more openly our own desires, [James A. Walsh] recognized our sincerity and earnestness of purpose and fostered our plans."[5]

Concluding her remarks, Mother Mary Joseph reiterated Bishop James Edward Walsh's convictions about women in mission, which were identical to hers. From her youthful years at Smith College when she first experienced her own call to mission, she dreamed of going overseas herself. Later, during her first two visits to the Sisters in South China she had become convinced that the women's role was akin to that of the early apostles. Maryknoll Sisters were called to an apostolic vocation. As early as 1929 she had begun to teach the younger Sisters that they were "all called to be apostles . . . each with the gifts God has given [you], to use for his purpose."[6] Mother Mary Joseph's model was St. Paul, the apostle commissioned by God through Christ and sent into the highways and byways to proclaim the good news of God's reign. She was aware that there were many ministries for the Sisters in foreign missions: education, health, and social assistance of all kinds. Regardless, she insisted that all ministries were to be grounded in the apostolic mission of sharing the gospel message in word and in witness. James E. Walsh's talk had unequivocally affirmed her long-held conviction that direct contact with the people had always been "dearest to my heart."[7]

The delegates reelected Mother Mary Joseph for another six-year term, hardly imagining how much heavier the burden of leadership was to become. The Sisters also did not suspect that they would not be able to gather for another General Chapter until 1946. In August 1937, as they began to return to their various missions, war clouds etched the horizon. While Germany was invading country after country in Europe, Japan tested its might against China. As populated areas in China came under Japanese control, travel and the means of communication were seriously disrupted.[8] The world was being catapulted into the Second World War.

The limited news that reached Maryknoll at this time weighed heavily on Mother Mary Joseph. Letters from Maryknollers in China rarely reached Hong Kong, let alone the United States. However, what was happening in each Maryknoll area was being faithfully recorded in mission diaries that would make for gripping community reading in the postwar years. Mother Mary Joseph wrote her Sisters during Lent of 1938 about the violent situation and resulting lack of communication:

> Those of you in troubled sections are continually in my thoughts and prayers. I have had no word from Shanghai since November and from our dear ones there. The Perpetual Adoration now going on as part of our daily life affords me the greatest consolation—for I know that day and night you are being continuously placed under God's loving care and the special protection of our Lady.[9]

Immediately after the 1937 General Chapter, Mother Mary Joseph had planned a trip to Hawaii and Asia to see personally how the Sisters were faring. She understood the importance of having direct contact with the Sisters, especially during times of war, but she was denied a passport by the State Department. Then, in the fall of 1938 and continuing into 1939, Mother Mary Joseph suffered a series of illnesses that culminated in surgery and a long recuperation. Finally, in the spring of 1940 she experienced renewed vigor and decided to set out with her sister, Sister Mary James Rogers, to visit the Sisters in mission on the West Coast, Hawaii, and, hopefully, Asia. Although she had doubts about reaching Asia, she was determined to make an attempt.[10] She would be successful to a point.

After visiting the various Maryknoll schools, social services, and catechetical programs in Hawaii, the two Sisters sailed for Asia. The ship made two brief stops in Japan and another in Shanghai. In each port, despite the prewar tension, the Sisters were able to spend a few hours with Mother Mary Joseph on board ship. They talked about a possible plan to follow as they faced the growing violence of war and the constraints on foreigners. The next stop was the British Colony of Hong Kong, the first of the missions in Asia (1921), where Mother Mary Joseph witnessed the dreadful plight of the refugees from mainland China and recorded some of the scenes in her diary:

> Hong Kong and Kowloon are filled with refugees and while the government does all it can to shelter and feed them it is impossible to care for all and the consequent suffering and poverty is unbelievable. Never have I dreamed human beings could go on living under such conditions—poorly clad, with only occasional food, and living and sleeping in the open.[11]

In Hong Kong, Mother Mary Joseph visited the two large schools the Sisters had established.[12] Living in the shadow of the Sino-Japanese war, the Sisters hoped their efforts and all the other projects they had initiated to meet the needs of the colony—soup kitchens, clinics, food and clothing distribution, training of emergency volunteers, teaching catechism, visiting hospitals—would not grind to a halt, especially in this time of overwhelming need.

From Hong Kong, Mother Mary Joseph proceeded to the Philippines, the fifth country of overseas mission for the Maryknoll Sisters. Once again she was gratified by all that the Sisters had accomplished. However, the future appeared ominous. In the midst of widespread rumors of all-out war she counseled the Sisters to keep their hearts focused on God's faithfulness regardless of the odds.

> What the New Year holds for us we cannot even dimly see—so hidden are the designs of God these days. . . . I would urge each and every one to try through a lively and perfect submission of will, to make [her own] *Behold the handmaid of the Lord. Be it done to me, according to thy word.* Let this be more than ever our watch word, and a light to our souls.[13]

Although Mother Mary Joseph had hoped to visit the Sisters in all the missions, the encroaching war made this impossible. She cabled the northern missions of China, Manchuria, and Korea from Manila, and the Sisters who were able to do so traveled to the port cities for a brief visit aboard ship, just as the Sisters from Japan and Shanghai had done. No matter how brief these visits were, the memory of Mother Mary Joseph's loving and serene presence sustained the Sisters all through the war years.[14]

6

World War II, 1941–1945

The early months of 1941 unfolded "like the tightening of a screw."[1] As war news from Asia and Europe seeped through the media, Mother Mary Joseph faced a very difficult decision: In this time of war, should the Maryknoll Sisters remain in their Asian missions? The tradition in the Catholic Church was that missioners remained with the people to whom they had been sent, regardless of cost or pain. Maryknollers took this for granted. The United States government, however, was advising its nationals to leave Asia in order to avoid internment as enemy aliens. Trusting in God's providence, and after consultation with local church authorities, Mother Mary Joseph decided the Sisters would stay in their missions.[2] She wrote many letters of encouragement and concern, especially to those she had not seen on her visitation the year before, hoping that somehow the letters would reach them.

By December 1941, within a year of her visit, the Japanese army invaded and took control of Manila, terminating all the missions and the outreach activity of the Maryknoll Sisters in the Philippines. On Christmas Day the island of Hong Kong was taken, and forty-nine Maryknollers, priests, Brothers, and Sisters, were placed in the Stanley Internment Camp with several thousand other prisoners of American, British, and Dutch nationalities. In view of drastic food shortages, the Japanese were eager to be rid of any prisoners who had no particular political or military value. Thus, by June 1942 thirty-one Maryknoll Sisters, a group of Maryknoll Fathers and Brothers, and other prisoners of war from Hong Kong, Manchuria, and Korea were exchanged for Japanese nationals. The Maryknollers arrived in New York on August 25, 1942, after a long and perilous voyage. Before August of that same year, 568 allied ships had been sunk.

While some Maryknollers were repatriated, others continued to be at risk in China and the Philippines. After the war the community would be held spellbound by the stories that were told, testaments to the uncommon faith, courage, and dedication of their fellow missioners. Thirty-eight Maryknoll Sisters in China had been constantly on the run from their pursuers and had resolutely continued their work under makeshift circumstances, suffering the same privations as the people they served. Two Sisters in the Philippines were captured, accused as spies, and tortured, while forty-seven others were forced to endure the hardships of internment camp in the Philippines together with over two thousand other foreigners.

Because most of the missioners in China and the Philippines had no idea which way the war was going, it seemed to them that their nightmare had no end. And the nightmare was as unbearable for those who longed to have news of them. After the first exchange of prisoners in August 1942, Mother Mary Joseph received little information about her Sisters in war-torn Asia until the release of thirty-two more the following year. She did her best to follow the distant war, but the ordinary channels of communication with all who remained behind enemy lines were blocked for the remainder of the war.

On January 6, 1945, the thirty-third anniversary of the arrival of the first three women at Hawthorne, Mother Mary Joseph gave a very moving meditation in which she expressed her deep concern. *"Many of our Sisters are far from us—many of them in peril, many of them working against great odds."* Not wanting to burden the community with her worries, she buoyed up their spirits with her confidence in their companions' indomitable fortitude. *"All are persevering in spite of obstacles and are cooperating beautifully with God's grace. . . . We think of them all. Our hearts, love, and prayers reach out to them."*[3]

Mother Mary Joseph was also very much aware of the suffering of the Japanese people in the United States, many of them U.S. citizens yet treated as enemy aliens and confined in internment camps for the duration of the war. In keeping with their missionary vocation, several Maryknoll Sisters, some of whom were Japanese Americans, stayed with the people with whom they had been working on the West Coast and followed them into internment camps rather than retreating to the relative comfort and safety of Maryknoll, New York.

In the course of the war Mother Mary Joseph neither worried over destroyed mission works in Asia nor allowed the life of the growing community to stagnate while awaiting better days. Although she was afflicted by recurring bouts of malaria, a heart condition, and an esophageal hernia, she continued to shoulder her responsibilities as leader of the Congregation. Characteristically, she was planning the reconstruction of the Asian missions at the same time that she was preparing to send Sisters to Latin America to join the Maryknoll priests and Brothers who had gone to the jungles of Bolivia in April of 1942.

The Sisters were in Bolivia and Panama within a year. Missions in Nicaragua followed in 1944.

In her solicitude for those in need, Mother Mary Joseph's mission vision extended also to minority groups in the United States. Schools were opened for African American children in St. Louis and New York City, while a mission served the Hispanic population in Guadalupe, California. More schools and missions were to follow. Mother Mary Joseph believed that these works established within the boundaries of the United States were just as truly missionary as those overseas, for all needed the loving care of the church.

On the Congregation's twenty-fifth jubilee, February 14, 1945, Mother Mary Joseph ended her conference to the Sisters with a solemn reflection:

> Today we are a strong, vigorous religious body [seven hundred Sisters] with far-flung missions. We see much of our work, built up through the years of toil and hardship and at great cost, now apparently in ruin. God alone knows why this is so. . . . Our task on this anniversary day is unchanged. We have only to persevere . . . placing our all in [God's] keeping, for *Unless the Lord build the city, they labor in vain that build it* (Ps 127).[4]

Fourteen days later, long awaited news finally came: the Sisters had been released from internment camp in the Philippines. One can only imagine the ecstatic joy and relief of Mother Mary Joseph and all the Sisters. It would be several more weeks before news was heard of six other Sisters, three in Manila and three in the northern city of Baguio. Toward the end of March, all of them had been accounted for except one, Sister Hyacinth Kunkel. She was one of nearly five hundred refugees who had to cross giant ridges and stumble through heavy torrents to reach safety. At one point she paused for a drink of water, and then she was simply not there. Although many guides searched the area relentlessly, no trace was ever found of her.[5] On June 13, 1945, Mother Mary Joseph wrote to the community: "As yet no definite word on our dear Sister Hyacinth. We accept the fact of death now but we still hope to find her precious remains."[6] Mother Mary Joseph's hope never materialized.

As the year 1945 drew to a close, Mother Mary Joseph, now sixty-three years old, remembered not only the recent years of World War II, but also the whole span of years since she had joined Fathers Walsh and Price in the beginnings of Maryknoll. She had arrived at Hawthorne on September 9, 1912, and on September 15 she had assumed the responsibility of leadership among the little group of "secretaries," a group she was to lead to full recognition as a religious congregation of missionary women by the church in 1920. The approaching year, 1946, would be the silver anniversary of the first group to make their vows. She had been the faithful, charismatic, and compassionate leader of the Maryknoll Sisters for thirty-three years. She was recognized and dearly loved as the founder of the Maryknoll Sisters' Congregation, a dedicated woman who had been deeply involved in the very foundation of Maryknoll. At this point in her life she remained stalwart and full of life, despite her chronic illnesses.

Mother Mary Joseph expressed the joy that filled her heart and the hearts of the Sisters in a meditation given in the chapel on Christmas Eve 1945. In her prayerful reflection she spoke of the state of the world, the sorrows of the war years, and the grace and challenges of their missionary vocation:

> The world at large knows today a peace and good will that have been withdrawn for a long, long time from the face of the earth. . . . Our Sisters in the Orient, though still suffering many privations, are safe once more. Sister Hyacinth we confidently leave in the merciful hands of God. . . . We should remember that our missionary vocation is essentially a work of great expectations and lively hope, calling for virtue of high order, practiced in heroic degree, whether we are here or in fields afar. . . . Let nothing, then, ever discourage us unduly, but daily expecting the birth and re-birth of Christ in our own souls and in those of our charges . . . assured that all will come to pass according to our expectations. The coming of Christ and the Christmas season confirm our hopes. So without fear, let us "prepare the way for the Lord."[7]

7

God Has Yet a Great Work
for Us to Do

Mother Mary Joseph's Christmas Eve conference might have served well as the opening talk at the fourth General Chapter, which in normal circumstances would have been held in 1943. She had postponed the chapter rather than hold such an important meeting without the participation of the missioners in Asia and the Pacific Islands.

Finally, in 1946, with the war's end, Mother Mary Joseph called the General Chapter for July 13, 1946. In her letter of convocation she pointed out the need to reorganize the work in order to meet the demands of reconstruction after the war.[1] She was also keenly aware that this was a new historical moment filled with hope for a peaceful world and new possibilities in mission throughout the world. Maryknollers were challenged not only to reconstruct their missions in Asia but also to widen and deepen their mission vision in light of their overseas experience. Maryknoll had recently begun missions in Latin America and would soon turn to East Africa.

In her introductory remarks at the General Chapter, Mother Mary Joseph stressed that the Congregation's spiritual beauty and ability to accomplish good works for God depended on the virtue and disciplined activity of each member. She quoted an entire talk given by Bishop Ford in which he interpreted Father James Anthony Walsh's ideal qualities of the Maryknoll Sister, giving a vivid description of each of the four qualities most needed in a missionary context: simplicity with singleness of vision, unmeasured generosity, calm cheerfulness, and forgetfulness of self. Mother Mary Joseph was convinced that the holiness of each missioner sustained the entire missionary movement.[2]

Once again, the Sisters unanimously reelected Mother Mary Joseph. This necessitated that a special request, known as a postulation, be sent to Rome for approval. Mother Mary Joseph had led the community since 1912. Normally, canon law permitted only two consecutive terms for a superior general. However, in 1937, Rome had approved her reelection readily, so by 1946 she had already served three consecutive terms. The chapter delegates assumed that, in the case of a founder, approval would be granted without question.

At the conclusion of the chapter Mother Mary Joseph delayed sending out the chapter report, expecting that an answer regarding the postulation would momentarily come from Rome. By October 26, 1946, with still no word, she presented a summary of the chapter's discussions and conclusions in a detailed letter to the community. Among the areas mentioned was the simplification of the Sisters' prayer life:

> I feel, and I trust without presumption, that, while still following whatever schedules are necessary for order in our work and personal discipline, the time is ripe for simplifying our life of prayer and cultivating a truer liberty of soul, by which we may reach out at will towards God and not be hampered by an over-regimented, parceled-out prayer life.[3]

She recognized that the very heart of their religious life as a community was the Eucharist and the Divine Office. For Maryknollers interned during the war, these had been "the pearl of great price."[4] However, she had come to realize that mission life mandated occasions when the time available for prayer would be cut short by extenuating circumstances. In her letter she displayed both her trust in the integrity of each individual Sister and her wisdom in regard to prayer, carefully delineating that her objective was to give each Sister the responsibility of substituting a briefer prayer when necessary. It was characteristic of Mother Mary Joseph to trust the Sisters rather than legislate from fear of abuse.

On the first Sunday of Advent, December 1, 1946, Mother Mary Joseph called the community together to convey the news that the previous day the archbishop of New York, Francis Cardinal Spellman, had called her in to speak about the postulation, saying that he knew it would not be granted.

> [The Cardinal] advised me, very kindly, and with consideration of all our interests, to refuse the election and call an Elective chapter. This, of course, I will do, for an opinion of this kind should be law to us, who are subject to authority. While this act will take from my hands the government of the Congregation, it will also free me for things I have long wished to do and which should be of lasting help and benefit to us all.[5]

Speaking as mother foundress rather than mother general, she thanked the Sisters for their love, their loyalty, and their selfless cooperation from the beginning, adding that it had been an inexpressible joy to serve them.

One month later the delegates gathered again to choose her successor. In her address to them Mother Mary Joseph spoke about authentic obedience, which never robs a person of freedom or stifles a human choice of action. She firmly believed that if we accepted the inevitable events in our lives as somehow part of God's plan for us, then our reaching out to God made us victors, not slaves under the law. It was her moment to reach out freely and embrace a new time in her life and in the life of the Congregation.[6] Mother Mary Joseph's concluding words reverberate in the heart of every Maryknoll Sister:

> Love, work, prayer, and suffering will sustain us in the future as they have in the past. All who are here now, all who will come after us will have no other tools than these with which to build. . . . God has yet a great work for us to do. . . . But the realization of this vision depends on you and me as individuals and on our cooperation. Do we love enough, do we work enough, do we pray enough, do we suffer enough? Maryknoll's future depends on our answer.[7]

That same morning Sister Mary Columba Tarpey was elected mother general. In a letter that followed, Mother Mary Joseph expressed her confidence in the new mother general: "Knowing Mother Mary Columba's character intimately as I do, I am content to leave you to her loving prayerful solicitude and her wise devoted care."[8]

Mother Mary Joseph's first decision as mother founder was based on practical wisdom. She thought it best to leave the Motherhouse for a while, giving Mother Mary Columba the space and time to establish herself as the new leader of the Congregation. In her new role in a community called to mission, Mother Mary Joseph wanted to continue her work for the formation of the Sisters. Despite her frequent periods of ill health, she wanted to be totally available to the Sisters for their spiritual and human growth. Mother Mary Joseph gave a retreat to the canonical novices, bade goodbye to all at Maryknoll and the New York area, and then in mid-February 1947 settled for some months at the Maryknoll Sanatorium in Monrovia, California.[9]

In October, at Mother Mary Columba's request, she moved to the newly opened novitiate in Valley Park, Missouri. There was some apprehension in the community regarding how both the Maryknoll spirit and unity could be fostered and maintained away from the Motherhouse. Mother Mary Joseph was very supportive of this project, which was Mother Mary Columba's first major decision. She saw it as necessary in view of the numbers who were entering and counseled everyone not to worry about the spirit, which, if genuine, would remain, because the spirit resided in each individual Sister.

> Every sister who touches the novitiate in any way must give the example of our Maryknoll way of life—a way marked by simplicity, spiritualized naturalness and individuality, and consciousness of the indwelling of Christ, from which flow religious dignity and the all-embracing love of one another and of all outside our family circle. It is for you and for me to preserve this spirit.[10]

In the ensuing months Mother Mary Joseph gave retreats to the Sisters at the Motherhouse, in Valley Park, in Monrovia, and in Hawaii. She then settled in Monrovia once again in the fall of 1948, making it the center from which she visited all the missions in California. She was clearly a missioner to her missionary Sisters, encouraging, challenging, and strengthening their call to build God's reign in the world.[11]

In March 1949, Mother Mary Joseph felt it was time for her to return to the Motherhouse to stay. She did not intend to end her work but to undertake three writing projects that were constantly being urged on her: the story of Maryknoll's beginnings, the story of the founders, and her own vocation story. In between the many calls on her time and energy, she tried to do these projects, but ultimately, all three projects would be left to Maryknoll posterity.[12]

The year 1950 opened up a new time of life for Mother Mary Joseph as she settled into life at the Motherhouse. On various community occasions she gave significant meditations to the community that led the Sisters into a greater understanding and appreciation of their call as women religious in mission. She focused her presentations on keeping alive the history of the Maryknoll Sisters, their spiritual heritage, their call to the foreign missions, the quality of their community life, and their personal growth in holiness.[13]

In June 1950 Mother Mary Joseph spent a week at her alma mater, Smith College, where she celebrated the forty-fifth anniversary of her graduation and received the honorary degree of Doctor of Humane Letters. She had declined this honor twice before, in 1940 and in 1943, because of ecclesiastical objections. Now that she had been given permission, her acceptance gave public witness to the influence and inspiration that Protestant students and teachers at Smith had played in her missionary call.[14] Mother Mary Joseph rejoiced in these honors because she knew they were also in recognition of the whole Congregation.

In 1951, while Mother Mary Joseph continued her usual activity and involvement at the Motherhouse, Maryknoll missioners in Asia were being severely tested once again. Maryknollers had returned to their missions after the war, filled with enthusiasm and renewed hope for the future, never suspecting that their mission to the people of China would be thwarted once again. By 1947, the Communists were exerting control over more and more territory, and by 1950 all missioners in China were systematically arrested, imprisoned, and/or expelled.[15]

Korea faced the same upheaval and terror during the postwar years. After World War II, the only Maryknoll Sister left in North Korea was Sister Agneta Chang. She was from an illustrious Korean family that had been Catholic since the nineteenth century. In 1932, she and three other Maryknoll Sisters were given the responsibility of establishing a Korean congregation dedicated to Our Lady of Perpetual Help. When her companions, all foreigners, were repatriated, Sister Agneta continued the formation and direction of the Sisters until her death in October 1950. Sister Peter, a member of the Sisters of Perpetual Help, wrote a long letter to Mother Mary Joseph describing the circumstances of Sister Agneta's death. She wrote that the Communists came at night and threw Sister Agneta into an oxcart. It was believed that she was shot that same night and buried in a mass grave.[16] Seven weeks after her death Maryknoll's Bishop Patrick J. Byrne died in the notorious Korean "Death March."

In the spring of 1951 Mother Mary Joseph began to get news of the Sisters in South China as they crossed the border into Hong Kong a few at a time. Each Sister carried her story of Communist hostility and accusations. Some had endured long weeks under house arrest, and several had suffered frightful days and nights in Communist prisons. In April, Bishop Francis X. Ford and his secretary, Sister Joan Marie Ryan, were arrested. By winter it was obvious that at this moment of history, the Maryknoll missions, as well as all other Christian missions in China, were coming to a tragic end. Mother Mary Joseph's anguish is palpable in this talk in December 1950:

> I thought when we went through the last dreadful siege of internment for our own Sisters in the Philippines, in China, Manchuria, wherever they were, that my heart could never bleed again as it did

during those months, even years of anxiety. And yet today we find ourselves even more cruelly upset, more tortured by the thought of what is happening to our dear ones.[17]

On March 23, 1952, Mother Mary Joseph suffered a severe stroke that was further complicated by her medical history.[18] However, after long months of therapy coupled with a determined spirit, she regained enough motion to sit in a wheelchair and enjoy a tour of the Maryknoll compound in the back of an open truck—but she was never able to walk again.[19]

8

As One Lamp Lights Another

During the last few years of her life Mother Mary Joseph remained physically fragile, yet she retained her gracious disposition and spontaneous good humor until the end. She remained courageous and outgoing with all who came to see her and with those whom she met in her wheelchair adventures. She also managed to send out at least three substantial letters to Maryknoll Sisters around the world during 1952, 1953, and 1954. These long, newsy letters communicated Motherhouse happenings and also continued her words of spiritual formation, inspiration, and encouragement. Her last letter of July 30, 1954, the feast of the Sacred Heart, was a particularly moving as she described the appreciation and gratitude for the gift the Sisters were to her:

> One day, I leaned back—closed my eyes and just thought of you all around the globe. Over the years, my mind roamed—and, at every turn, you were there—sustaining and encouraging me, working shoulder to shoulder with me. So, it is today such a joy to know that wherever there are Maryknoll Sisters there is peace and cooperation and lovely, boundless charity. . . . Only very occasionally is this beauty marred by a selfish, self-centered few for whom I pray most earnestly.[1]

As soon as spring arrived in 1955, Mother Mary Joseph was outdoors as much as possible. But when the heat of summer descended on the Knoll, she became noticeably tired, beginning to have moments of preoccupation and withdrawal from what was happening around her.

On October 3, 1955, Mother Mary Joseph visited the contemplative community of Maryknoll Sisters on the hill overlooking the Motherhouse. On October 4 she went to the chapel, where she prayed her hour of Adoration—a community devotion she had initiated many years before. The day of October 5 started well, but by evening she became very weak. Her condition worsened until it became necessary to hospitalize her in the wee hours of October 8. By afternoon of the following day she could hardly speak. Mother Mary Columba described the moment of her passing very simply: "We all prayerfully waited for God's call, which came quietly after a few short struggles for breath at 5:18 P.M." Mother Mary Joseph Rogers died on October 9, 1955.[2]

Forty-five years earlier, on September 15, 1910, Mollie Rogers had made a formal resolve to devote her entire life to the foreign mission initiative that would soon become known as Maryknoll. Over those many years she had given herself entirely—body, mind, heart, and spirit—to the foundation of this missionary movement, the first of its kind among Catholics in the United States.

One of her most outstanding gifts during her many years of leadership was the profoundly spiritual yet deeply human formation for mission that she gave the Maryknoll Sisters. She often described what she called the Maryknoll spirit as naturalness of manner, frankness, and openness. For her Sisters she put forth this ideal: "I would have her distinguished by Christ-like charity, a limpid simplicity of soul, heroic generosity, selflessness, unfailing loyalty, prudent zeal, gracious courtesy, an adaptable disposition, solid piety, and the saving grace of a kindly humor."[3]

Together, the Sisters were to form a strongly bonded community of apostolic women, wholly committed to the following of Jesus in his mission to the world. As a gracious guide with a unique vision of the mission vocation, she enjoined each Sister to be responsible for the common good of the whole Congregation. "If you love Maryknoll . . . you will put aside self-love and self-interests . . . [and will] give to one another that beautiful gift, especially charity."[4] She carefully shaped this Maryknoll spirit through her conferences and letters, the reading she encouraged, and her own relationships with the Sisters, being wont to quote, "As one lamp lights another, nor grows less, so nobleness enkindleth nobleness."[5]

9

Epilogue

By the time of Mother Mary Joseph's death on October 9, 1955, the Maryknoll Sisters' Congregation had 1,160 professed members. There had been an average increase of thirty-three Sisters a year for the previous thirty-five years. No one foresaw—and this was true for all congregations in the United States—that after Vatican II the influx of vocations would slow to a trickle.

Now, in 2012, one hundred years after the founding of the Maryknoll Sisters, the Congregation has fewer than five hundred professed members. A detailed treatment of the factors that account for this dramatic decrease is beyond the scope of this book. For our purposes, a brief look at the momentous changes that occurred, particularly those within the church during the last half of the twentieth century, offers a lens with which to view the profound transformation that has taken place in many apostolic religious congregations.

Even before Mother Mary Joseph's death the winds of change had begun to stir in religious life. In the early 1950s Pope Pius XII startled religious communities by calling them to rejuvenate themselves and to ensure that their young members would be well prepared both theologically and professionally. He encouraged the Sisters to discard outmoded customs and clothing that estranged them from the people they served.[1] After centuries of the church insisting on a monastic structure for active religious, including religious garb and restricted access to "the world," the Sisters were understandably bewildered by this call. But the seeds of change had been planted.

In 1956, the Sisters in the United States launched their far-reaching response in the Sister Formation Movement, which sought "to develop vowed women intellectually, psychologically, and spiritually in a setting of service."[2] At the very least it provided intensive theology and scripture classes for an additional year after first profession of vows. Despite the pressing needs in the missions, Maryknoll Sisters grasped the wisdom and potential of the Sister Formation Program. In the early

1960s, as soon as the program could be implemented, whole groups of twenty or thirty were held back from the mission field for a year in which to deepen their understanding of their apostolic religious life.

On the eve of the Second Vatican Council, Cardinal Suenens of Belgium stoked the fire with his groundbreaking book *The Nun in the World*.[3] Both Pope Pius and Cardinal Suenens recognized the formidable potential in the thousands of Sisters the world over. The Second Vatican Council (1962–65) followed immediately with its breadth of openness to the world, calling on religious to return to the original purpose of their institutes.

Sisters everywhere enthusiastically took up the challenges of Vatican II, many of them surprised by the refreshing vision of their founders. They rewrote their constitutions, insisting now that these documents inspire rather than circumscribe. As a result, the "daughters of the Church," convinced that "religious life today is not a relic of an age that is past, but a compelling, ongoing, evolving way of living the Gospel,"[4] were arguably the most ready and eager to implement the astounding insights of Vatican II.

The Vatican-inaugurated initiatives that were to transform religious life eventually took Vatican officials unaware. The Sisters had taken Rome at its word and, in the spirit of their founders, were making the changes necessary to be a relevant force in the world. In the United States it could be said that the shape the initiatives assumed as they evolved and were inculturated in the various religious communities reflected the Sisters' internalized democratic cultural values. For Maryknoll Sisters, and many other congregations where the members were becoming far more socially astute and fearless in addressing inequities, it was a short step to a horizontal style of leadership. This change, probably more than any other, disoriented the hierarchical character of Catholic Church officials, who were used to having the last word in all matters pertaining to the lives of women religious.

Not all the objections came from the Vatican, however. It was no simple matter to replace the centuries-old monastic forms that were no longer deemed appropriate for apostolic religious. During the years of "experimentation,"[5] disagreement on perceived essentials frequently put Sisters at odds with one another, and many withdrew from their congregations. While the changes that came after Vatican II were much too fast for some, they were too little and too late for others.

The turbulent happenings in religious life during the decades in question reflected the seismic shifts in a world culture precipitated by world wars and the global movements that relentlessly swept across cultures, some casting ominous shadows, others releasing prodigious energy for good. From the women's revolution to quantum leaps in medicine and communication technology to terrorism's mass crippling of civilizations, the twentieth-century generated an endless list of imponderables that changed the world forever.

From the life of Mother Mary Joseph, we now turn to the beginning of the twentieth century to look in broad strokes at the factors that converged to create the favorable conditions for the birth of Maryknoll.

Part II

Foundations of
Mother Mary Joseph's
Mission Vision

10

The American Foreign Mission
Context at the Turn
of the Twentieth Century

Before Mother Mary Joseph actually came to Maryknoll, the topic of foreign mission kept arising in her life, even when she was not particularly focused on it. Her initial fervent pledge in 1904 was not followed by specific steps that would lead her directly to mission work, and yet the dream took root in her heart. Over time, the dream became compelling enough for her to dedicate her entire life to foreign mission. How did this happen? Before attempting to describe the development of Mother Mary Joseph's mission vision, it may be helpful to glance at the "missiological environment" that constituted the state of mission in the United States at the end of the nineteenth century. We begin with an overview of the mission dynamism of the American Protestant churches, which had a decided influence on Mother Mary Joseph.

In the United States of America the missionary movement of the Protestant churches preceded that of the Catholic Church by nearly one hundred years. In 1810, a group of students at Andover Theological Seminary petitioned the General Association of Congregational Churches to initiate a society for overseas missions. The result was the organization of the American Board of Commissioners for Foreign Missions. Interdenominational in nature, it was the first organized attempt to recruit foreign missionaries in the United States. Two years later, five Protestant missionary couples sailed for India.

As the nineteenth century progressed, interest and support for missions grew steadily among Protestants. Initially, they concentrated on "home mission," intent on evangelizing the marginalized groups at the borders of Anglo-Saxon society, Native Americans, Hispanics, African Americans, and the many immigrant populations.[1]

In the final decades of that century, denominational boards with a clear focus on foreign missions proliferated. From fifteen boards by the end of the Civil War in 1865, there were ninety-six boards in 1910, with 7,219 Protestant missionaries, husbands and wives, serving overseas.[2]

Concomitant with this astounding development, single Protestant women quickly developed a feminine movement of their own:

> Early nineteenth-century women seldom wrote theologies of mission, but they wrote letters and kept journals that reveal a rich thought world and a set of assumptions about women's roles in the missionary task. . . . A phalanx of unmarried women built upon the efforts of the missionary wives and carried out works of education, medicine, and evangelism. . . . Women became the majority among the mission force as well. Their commitment to the social and charitable side of mission transformed the face of American missions.[3]

While Protestant efforts in mission were motivated by a love for Christ and the salvation of souls, they were also mixed with the sociopolitical ideals of the era.

> Underneath . . . was the compelling idea, developing since the 1840s, of America's Manifest Destiny—of a national mission assigned by Providence for extending the blessings of America to other peoples. . . . Until the 1890s Manifest Destiny was thought of primarily in terms of continental expansion, of "winning the West," with the absorption of settlers into citizenhood and statehood. In the 1890s, however, when the United States had reached the limits of prospective continental expansion, there developed agitation for expansion beyond North America.[4]

In the 1880s, an amazing burst of energy erupted as a result of the inspired ministry and contagious enthusiasm for mission of leading Protestant ministers such as Arthur Tappan Pierson (1837–1911).[5] Pierson was a New York Presbyterian pastor distinguished in the fields of biblical studies and pastoral ministry. Drawn to the needs of the urban poor, in 1881 he initiated a ministry to the unchurched. This experience awakened him irrevocably to the worldwide mission of the church. In 1886, he published the major work of the missionary era, *The Crisis of Christian Missions; or the Voice Out of the Cloud.* That same year, to the 251 students from about ninety colleges gathered at the Mount Hermon Summer Conference in Northfield, Massachusetts, he gave a talk focused on the great need for foreign missions. His message, "All shall go and shall go to all," so fired the students' imagination and ideals that one hundred of them signed up for foreign missionary service before they left the conference. The "Mount Hermon 100" became the nucleus for one of the most remarkable missionary movements in the United States—the Student Volunteer Movement for Foreign Missions (SVM).

By the time Pierson died in 1911, over five thousand student volunteers had served as foreign missionaries. John Mott, one of the students who had been deeply inspired by Pierson's galvanizing message at the Mount Hermon Conference, went on to head the SVM, the Young Men's Christian Association (YMCA), and also to serve as honorary president in the World Council of Churches. In his leadership capacities he gave full credit to Pierson for the SVM watchword, "The Evangelization of the World in This Generation," and popularized it further in his own classical text of 1900, *History of the Student Volunteer Movement for Foreign Missions.*

Mott explained that the SVM's intent was not the wholesale conversion of the world before the second coming of Christ, as trumpeted by premillennialists. Rather, it accented "giving to all people an adequate opportunity of knowing Jesus Christ as their Savior and of becoming His real disciples."[6]

At the same time that the SVM was flourishing in the Protestant missionary world, Mollie Rogers was a young student at Smith College (1901–5). An article in the January 1911 issue of *The Smith Alumnae Quarterly* describes the breadth of the missionary spirit she encountered there. Missionary awareness and commitment to overseas missions were part of the college's founding vision in 1875. Women were sent into mission within three years of the first graduation: "Of the thirty-nine missionaries who have gone out from Smith as alumnae or undergraduates, ten have worked in China or are now at work there; ten in Japan; ten in India; two in Syria; four in Asiatic Turkey; one in European Turkey; one in Colombia, South America; and one in Korea."[7]

These young missionaries represented eighteen of the thirty-two classes, ranging from 1882 to 1907, with the "banner" classes being 1900, with seven missionaries, and 1901, with five. Some of these Smith women gave long years of missionary service.[8] Upon their return, many took up mission work in the United States.

It is not surprising then that Mollie Rogers's early childhood attraction to foreign missions should have been reanimated at Smith. In the early spring of her junior year, 1904, Mollie presented one of the sessions of the Smith College Mission Study Classes.[9] This program of eight sessions from October to April was designed "to create an intelligent interest in Missionary work, through the study of some of the work done on the Home and Foreign Fields, its purpose, methods and results."[10] Mollie's class, last in the series, was probably the first ever at Smith on Catholic missions. Although she had meager resources, she proposed to cover an impressive amount of material:

> This class will study the work done by the Catholic Church in Home and Foreign Missions, in America, the Indian Schools, Leper Settlements and City Missions and the work of the Redemptorist, Jesuit and Paulist Fathers among Non-Catholics. It will study the Coast Missions in South America and Africa, emphasizing work done by Nuns, and the work in China, Japan and the Pacific Isles, with local studies of the most important missions.
>
> —Leader, Mary Rogers, 1905[11]

Two months after leading this study Mollie had a life-changing religious experience, one she often shared with others as the story of her earliest call to mission.

> It was a June evening, still, warm and sweet with the fragrance of the flowering campus. I was a junior in one of the largest non-sectarian colleges in the country, and, as I walked slowly towards the Students' Building from the Hall which had been home to me for three years, I dreamed in the manner of every girl of that age about the future, of what my part was to be in the betterment of the world. I would soon be a senior and a definite decision must be made.[12]

As she walked along, a little childhood prayer slipped into her thoughts: "Dear Jesus, grant that we may all drop down together, and please let me be a credit to my church."[13] It was a curious prayer she had made up as a young child when she had heard others talking about a Catholic who had been a source of scandal to the church. Mollie realized that although she had not failed in her duties as a child of the church, in reality she had done little to bring herself and others closer to God. And then,

> These wholesome reveries were suddenly broken by shouts of joy as the great doors of the Students' Building were flung open and floods of light poured out upon the paths. A crowd of girls rushed out and, before I realized what was happening, a circle had been formed of about five or six of them and the stirring strains of "Onward Christian Soldiers" were winging themselves over the campus.
>
> I soon learned that these girls had just signed the Student Volunteer pledge and that the following September would see them all on

the way to China, foreign missionaries. . . . They had signed a promise to the College Foreign Mission Board to go for seven years to China to teach in the mission schools or work in the hospitals. . . . Everybody in college knew what the Student Volunteer pledge meant for missionary activity was strong and I had often been asked to join the mission study classes and contribute to the mission fund, but this was [my] first experience in the actual offering of the young women and they were the College's best. . . . Something—I do not know how to describe it—happened within me. I forgot my errand; I was no longer mindful of the beauty and joy about me; I passed quickly through the campus, out of the college grounds, and across the street to the church where, before Jesus in the tabernacle, I measured my faith and the expression of it by the sight I had just witnessed. I was a Catholic and I had known from childhood that there were foreign mission societies which needed help; I had even had idle visions of working for the salvation of souls. The fact was that I had done nothing. I knew myself to be one of God's selfish children who had received much and given little in the way of an active service of love. And my friends . . . were going to China to lead pagan souls through paths of error to Christ! *From that moment, I had work to do, little or great, God alone knew.*[14]

Many years later, in the spring of 1953, Mother Mary Joseph remembered this moment as if it had happened yesterday: "That scene remained long with me and I wondered about Catholic missions and if there was a place for Catholic girls like myself in whom this mission interest was taking a very definite form of dedication, although the very thought of a religious vocation was abhorrent."[15]

Why Mollie had such an aversion to religious life is a matter of speculation. Aside from not having had much contact with women religious, if any at all, she was obviously not attracted to them and would therefore never have imagined religious life for herself. Only a few years later, however, through her work with Father James A. Walsh in the Boston office of the Society for the Propagation of the Faith, letters from missionaries inspired her and her perceptions began to change. But, as a student, what impressed her was the place her Protestant friends, young women like her, had in foreign mission. The obvious question came to her: If for Protestant women, why not also for Catholic lay women?

Throughout her life Mother Mary Joseph would speak of Smith College as one of the most significant influences in her missionary call. In a talk to the Newman Club at Columbia University in 1925 she went so far as to affirm that if it had not been for Smith College she might not have discovered her vocation.[16] Later, in a talk to the community, she said, "I love Smith College very much. . . . It was there that I got my vocation."[17] She credited the ardor for the Gospel in her non-Catholic companions as "the star" that guided her toward her life's work in mission.

From this brief consideration of how American Protestant zeal for foreign missions influenced Mollie's life, especially during her Smith years, we now turn to the influence of the Catholic Church in the United States. This was a time of the dawning of mission awareness among Catholics and the emergence of Maryknoll as the foreign mission enterprise of the United States Catholic hierarchy.

11

The Catholic Awakening

At the dawn of the twentieth century in the Roman Catholic Church, the United States was still considered mission territory. European missionaries had been coming to the New World since its discovery to evangelize and establish the church and to engage in works of mercy. They planted the seeds of faith at great cost to themselves, sometimes offering their lives. The heroic figures of Isaac Jogues, SJ, and Jean de Bréboeuf, SJ, were household names in Catholic families, as were Marie de l'Incarnation, OSU; Philippine Duchesne, RSCJ; Frances Cabrini, SMSC; Junipero Serra, OFM; and a host of others, most of whom were from Europe.[1] But there were signs that this imbalance would soon begin to change.

The World Parliament of Religions in Chicago in 1893, "an event that intertwined social issues, religious unity, ecumenism, and mission," generated a lot of excitement and assuredly contributed to Catholic America's "coming of age."[2] Paulist Father Walter Elliott (1842–1928) spoke at the Parliament, promoting a Catholic outreach to non-Catholics in the United States.[3] Subsequently, he and his confrere, Alexander Doyle (1857–1912), held mission conferences in 1904, 1906, 1908, and 1909 that brought together people who were "thinking and talking mission."

It is not surprising that from this interactive platform the foreign mission dream of James A. Walsh, director of the Society for the Propagation of the Faith in Boston, should flourish.[4] At the 1904 Mission Conference Walsh had given a talk on Catholic foreign missions. Thomas Frederick Price, a priest from North Carolina, had spoken on the progress of localized missions.[5] Correspondence between the two priests ensued. In 1910 they joined forces in the foundation of the Catholic Foreign Mission Society of America. Initially, however, Price was primarily concerned about local needs, while Walsh was convinced that the time had come for Americans to share in the worldwide mission of the church.[6]

Walsh continued his work in Boston and, together with three other priests, founded the Catholic Foreign Mission Bureau.[7] They set out to animate the missionary spirit among Catholics in the United States as well as to develop more reading materials on mission. From this venture, the first issue of *The Field Afar*, "an illustrated bi-monthly paper designed to interest all classes of people in Catholic missions," was published on January 1, 1907, with the able assistance of Mollie Rogers, who contributed her time and talents unreservedly.[8]

On January 29, 1908, a major impetus for Walsh's work and that of all mission-minded people in the United States occurred when Pope Pius X issued the apostolic constitution *Sapienti Consilio*.[9] This document dealt with a variety of matters, one of which was to declare that the Catholic Church in the United States had been removed from the jurisdiction of the Congregation of Propaganda Fide.[10] America was no longer regarded by the Holy See as mission territory. Effectively, the United States was placed on a basis of equality with the ancient churches of Europe. To Walsh and all others who shared his dream, this meant that the Catholic Church in the United States should hasten to join the universal mission effort by sending missioners of its own.

Even with the papal declaration, however, the assumption of responsibility for foreign missions was slow to take off in the United States. The dearth of mission literature and the all-absorbing needs of immigrant populations fostered insularity among Catholics.[11] Walsh was undeterred. Since his appointment as director of the mission office in Boston, he had insisted that "while charity begins at home, it should not end there. . . . Unless charity expands, it will die."[12] All along, he was confident that the mission spirit of the church in the United States would blossom once the country started sending out its own young missioners.

American Catholics benefited from the abundant literature and experience of Protestant missionaries as the conversation on foreign missions began. Even in the shadow of "Americanism,"[13] they quietly learned from the experience of Protestant missionaries, observed how they conducted their conferences, and profited by their example.[14] Mott's Student Volunteer Movement was probably in great part the inspiration for the Catholic Students' Mission Crusade.[15] The influence of the SVM on Mollie Rogers at Smith College has already been noted.

Although Walsh was totally dedicated to the foreign missions, he gave equal priority to home missions. He insisted they were not rivals, for Christ had come for all people.[16] His singular focus on foreign missions, however, can be traced to his seminary days in Brighton,

Massachusetts. His French Sulpician seminary professors instilled in him a keen interest in missionary activity by making him aware of the work of the French missioners in China and Indochina (Vietnam). Walsh was particularly inspired by the martyrs and tirelessly raised up to the young aspiring Maryknoll missioners the martyrdom of Théophane Vénard in Tonkin (Vietnam) in 1861. Yet, it was to the Paulist Fathers who worked in the American South that he gave credit for the strongest influence on the development of his missionary outlook.[17]

The Maryknoll founders, James Anthony Walsh, Thomas Frederick Price, and Mary Josephine Rogers, inspired by the lore of European missioners, particularly in China, placed their emphasis on the evocative images of the martyr and the fields afar.[18] To counter the dehumanizing elements of modern life, such as restlessness, loss of meaning, the "daily grind," they offered a bold and dynamic Christianity that appealed to young Catholics in the United States, opening them up to a whole new frontier.[19] The founders believed that the church in the United States was equal to the task of foreign mission.

12

Mollie's Path to Maryknoll

After graduating from Smith College in 1905, Mollie set her sights on higher education. In the fall of 1906 she became a demonstrator in zoology at Smith, a position that provided both valuable experience and the opportunity to begin work toward a master's degree. She might have pursued her dream of graduate studies had not a faculty member, Miss Elizabeth Deering Hanscom, unwittingly uttered the life-changing challenge that would set Mollie firmly on the path God had in mind for her, totally supplanting her pursuit of graduate study.[1] Having the good of the Catholic girls at heart, the teacher urged Mollie to do something for the Catholic students. Though somewhat diffident, Mollie agreed to start a mission study club. In the end it was not the study club in itself that altered Mollie's course in life, but all that it opened up for her in what followed.

Upon the advice of her confessor, she wrote James Anthony Walsh, director of the Society for the Propagation of the Faith (SPF) in Boston. Her letter reveals nothing of her wariness about what she might be embarking upon. Instead, it shows how much reflection she had done on the missions of the Catholic Church, how well organized she was, and most important, how interested she was. She probably surprised herself. Her letter reads in part:

> It has been for many years the custom among Protestant girls at this College to have what are known as Mission Study Classes in which they can discuss the work of the Protestant churches among the heathen. I have been asked to teach a class on Catholic missions.
>
> The particular motive of these classes is to inspire the girls to do actual work when they leave college. As Protestants have an abundance of material from which to draw, there are usually about ten classes—each occupied with a special part of the world. With us Catholics it will be quite different. By giving the girls what information we can get, we hope to show them how great the work of the

Church is, to make them want to keep in touch with that work and to give it their hearty support whenever an opportunity affords, now or later. The schedule as planned is as follows:

1st—The preparation of priest and nuns for the work.

2nd—Mission Orders and the Field of Work.

3rd—Nature of the work done.

4th—Collection and distribution of Funds.

Will you tell me where I can get any information (in English, French or Latin) bearing on these lines of thought? And will you kindly send me some pamphlets concerning the Society for the Propagation of the Faith? *Who knows but that the little work we do here may be the beginning of greater efforts in later life.*

—[signed Mary J. Rogers][2]

Although Mollie did not keep a copy of her first letter to Father Walsh, he did. He published part of it five months later in the May 1907 issue of his newly established mission magazine, *The Field Afar.* The anonymous author was presented as an example of what young Catholics could do to fire mission awareness in the church in the United States.

Father Walsh's answer of October 20, 1906, was a warm, encouraging reply—three typewritten pages—in which he carefully addresses all of her concerns about the classes. Without changing anything in her outline, he proposed that she add one subject: "The martyr spirit of our age . . . on which my mind and heart are so full." His letter reads in part:

My dear Miss Rogers,

Far from bothering me, your appeal gives me great pleasure in the thought that you will interest the Catholic girls of Smith College in the great work of Catholic Foreign Missions—a work which up to the present time, has not been appreciated by the Catholics of America, and which we have reason to believe is fast growing in popular favor. . . . I wish you were a little nearer, so that I could give some personal attention to this work *which I believe will be of far reaching importance, more so than you realize at the present moment.* . . .

Don't be afraid to write to me as often as you wish on the subject of this work. I shall look upon it as a privilege and pleasure to assist you in the effort which you are making and for which Almighty God will give you some reward through the prayers and sacrifices of those whom you are thereby helping.

Sincerely yours,

[signed James A. Walsh][3]

Walsh's response reflected his enthusiasm for her project. He immediately provided her with materials, and Mollie's fears abated. Walsh's letter was not merely an encouraging reply. In her mature years she was to recognize it as an answer to her silent prayer before the Blessed Sacrament in June 1904 when she grasped God's call to "an active service of love."[4] Years later she recalled that "the Catholic girls showed such an interest in the study club that almost every one of them was enrolled and attended most faithfully the meetings, held every Friday evening in the Students' Building. This study group finally turned into a Newman Club that persists today at Smith."[5]

Walsh also invited Mollie to involve herself in the work of the SPF office—translations, compilations, and other needed tasks. Walsh introduced her to *The Field Afar*, explaining that its purpose was to raise the consciousness of American Catholics, making them aware of their duty in the church's mission work. They needed to know about the missions, the requisites, accomplishments, martyrs, confessors, and finally, the need for a foreign mission seminary to train our own missioners.[6] It was time for Americans to take their place alongside their European counterparts. Mollie's eagerness to assist catapulted her into the wider world of Catholic missions.

During the summer of 1907 Mollie became a daily collaborator with Father Walsh. In the office he cleared a space for "Mollie's desk," where she translated mission material, edited articles, and organized the picture files for *The Field Afar*. In the spring of 1908 she finished her second year of teaching at Smith and set aside her personal plans for further education. She would teach at a school that was in close proximity to the SPF office so as to maximize the amount of time she could give to Walsh's project. On Christmas Eve of that same year Walsh gave her a Christmas gift, a bound copy of the first year's issues of *The Field Afar*. His inscription on the flyleaf, "To my co-worker with deep appreciation of her faithful service," attests to her steady, efficient contribution to the development of the new mission magazine.

In the following years Mollie's commitment intensified. As she participated in the development of Walsh's dream, it became her dream. When the Society was founded on June 29, 1911, she was fully committed to the success of this momentous project through a personal consecration she had made of her life on September 15, 1910.[7]

13

Mother Mary Joseph Rogers's Mission Vision

When Mollie came to Hawthorne in September 1912, she had no idea that the group Walsh was asking her to lead would evolve into a religious congregation. For her, becoming a missionary Sister was not fulfilling a lifelong dream. As already noted, she had never been attracted to religious life. She came, as did the others, to give her life to the mission project envisioned by Walsh. From the beginning, however, there seemed to have been an assumption among the other women that at some point they would become a recognized religious body.[1] For the time being, they were content to think of themselves as auxiliaries.[2] They concurred with James Anthony Walsh that their first obligation was to work for the development of the Society and only later, *if* the needs at home were adequately met, could they think of the possibility of also serving in foreign lands.[3] That was a big "if" in the early days, given the work entailed in the production of *The Field Afar*, the promotion of foreign mission vocations in the United States, and generally making known the work of Maryknoll. But the women grew in number and eventually received official recognition by the church as a bona fide congregation of women religious missioners. It was only a matter of time before they were to take their place alongside their Maryknoll Brothers in China.

Within a few days of her arrival, Mollie became Mary Joseph.[4] She had a minimal understanding and knowledge of the exigencies of the life she was making her own, even after committing herself totally. She was well educated, but the Sunday School classes she attended as a child were hardly sufficient to ground her in the Catholic culture that would have given her the breadth of knowledge she needed in her leadership of the group that would develop into a new religious congregation. From the vantage point of the twenty-first century, we look on with awe as we watch her move boldly into uncharted territory, relying on Divine Providence and on the guidance of James Anthony Walsh.

Of the three founders, Mother Mary Joseph did not come empty handed, though she was the least prepared theologically for the groundbreaking project of Maryknoll. From the Maryknoll Sisters who knew her and continue to regale the community with stories, and through her writings and taped conferences, she emerges as a highly intelligent woman, endowed with a gracious disposition, an abundance of common sense, a very generous heart, a clear Catholic identity, and most important of all, someone who had no doubt whatsoever that Maryknoll was God's work. She brought all of these qualities liberally to bear on her leadership and in her role as founder, enriching the whole Maryknoll enterprise immeasurably.

From the moment the congregation was established, before any of the Sisters really understood what cross-cultural mission involved, Mother Mary Joseph responded with her heart and assigned Sisters to work among the Japanese people on the West Coast. Within two years Sisters were also in South China. In 1923 she set out to "walk in the shoes of the China missioners," so to speak, because she knew that experience of the Sisters' reality firsthand would equip her to prepare the future missioners more adequately. She took meticulous notes so that the Sisters back home would learn along with her the requirements of mission life. Her 141 handwritten pages on this first mission visitation clearly indicate that she had eye-opening experiences, as she candidly admitted to Walsh: "Hitherto, I have, I realize now, viewed the whole mission life with the exaltation of the enthusiast, and I find myself appreciating for the first time, what perseverance in a vocation like ours entails. I look at [missionaries here and] our own loved ones . . . with reverence and admiration."[5]

Mother Mary Joseph made a second visitation in 1926 and 1927. Both this journey and the earlier one, several months in duration, steeped her in the vagaries of mission life. In her travels she met with other missionary communities and learned from them how they prepared their Sisters. As a keen observer, she could see immediately that good will and professional training were not enough. For the direct apostolate in China specifically, and to thrive in mission generally, the Sisters would need a much more thorough theological and scriptural foundation, in her view, "the same as for the priests."

Determined to strengthen the women's place in mission, in 1929 she formulated a Mission Policy based on the experience of her visitations.[6] Her phrasing of the policy indicates an undercurrent of allusions to the difficulties she had witnessed. The Sisters' lack of preparedness evidently accounted for friction between them and some of the priests. She confronted the reality with her characteristic humility, fully committed to amending situations rather than assuming a self-righteous stance. Although she knew truth was never totally on one side, she did not presume to correct what may have been a problem coming from the priests. The Sisters would look to their own shortcomings and address them as possible.

The opening paragraph of the Mission Policy is a sincere, unguarded, and positive approach to the problems and challenges of women missioners at that time:

> The Sisters' work in the missions needs for its satisfactory development a definite mission method on the part of the Sisters and a working plan based on their relation with the priests and bishop. We shall try to consider them in the order named, remembering that for their attainment, training and experience are required in the same measure in which they are required for the priests.

Mother Mary Joseph goes on to acknowledge the tension she feels in terms of adequately training Sisters for specific mission requirements such as direct evangelization and also staffing an increasingly busy Maryknoll Center, including the departments of both the Society and the Congregation. She affirms that while the work at home is no less valid, it is in fact "away from the mission field." Given the home requirements,

> only a few [Sisters] could be prepared directly for work in China, Korea, or elsewhere. Even when the Sisters went to the East they needed an adequate experience and a further training which, we have come to learn, requires from three to five years. The actual conditions in China were not such as to make the acquisition easy.

Well aware of the criticisms made concerning the Sisters—she had witnessed their legitimacy—she says clearly, "We hope to profit by them—though no one could have been more conscious than ourselves that we were student, not graduate, missioners." She then specifies five obstacles that militate against the development of the mission and the perseverance of the individual Sisters: "The difficulty of language acquirement, the social conditions of the country which limit the activity of women; the difficulty of financial support; the lack of a definite plan for Sisters' work; the numerous other obstacles common to any foreign undertaking, climate, etc." She ends this paragraph with her customary common sense: "These difficulties are formidable but they are such as might have been anticipated. They call for readjustment not withdrawal."

In light of her analysis of the mission experience of the Sisters, Mother Mary Joseph elaborates on two points. First, with rare exceptions, she specifies that in countries without a Christian tradition, "the Sisters shall be encouraged to undertake direct catechetical and evangelical work and for that purpose will expect to go from station to station for visitations comparable to those of the priest."

Second, she proposes a strategy to deal with the support of the Sisters. Rather than have the burden fall on one entity, she suggests that it be equitably shared by the Congregation, the Society, and the local bishop. The plan Mother Mary Joseph advanced placed realistic limits on mutual expectations with regard to financial obligations and also on accountability in the ministries.

As Mother Mary Joseph concludes the Mission Policy statement, she reflects on her conviction that Society and Congregation should work together where possible:

> There are many calls for the Sisters from other lands and the Sisters have succeeded creditably in such places as Manila, Honolulu and Hong Kong, yet I feel that the community needs, for the proper fulfillment of its purpose such mission works [direct evangelization] as China, Japan, Manchuria and Korea offer. Moreover, our primary interest in the field afar would naturally be the Maryknoll Missions just as our almost exclusive interest at home is with the Maryknoll Center and its works.

She then sincerely requests the recommendations of the addressees, Father James A. Walsh and the Society and Congregational superiors in China: "We would be glad to learn: (1) if our suggestions meet with your agreement, (2) what missions or works you might plan to entrust to the Maryknoll Sisters, (3) what suggestions you would offer to make our mutual work more successful, under the Providence of God."

It would be instructive to read some of the feedback Mother Mary Joseph most surely received regarding her inquiry, but no amount of searching in the Maryknoll Mission Archives has unearthed a single item. It may be that her initiative generated more appreciation than suggestions and that there was general agreement with the viability of her recommendations. Regardless, her strategy to garner the cooperation and ideas of all concerned seemed to diffuse the frustrations inherent in beginnings and to lead to a satisfactory outcome.

A committee of delegates at the General Chapter of 1931 worked on the policy, which was then incorporated into the Constitutions.[7] The text deals extensively with sources of support for the Sisters and how the Sisters were to be assimilated into the mission's plan and works, with mutual expectations carefully delineated. Mother Mary Joseph may have hoped that the policy would also cover the theological preparation of the Sisters. Was that what she intended by "experience and training . . . the same as for the priests?" If so, that aspect does not appear in the 1931 Constitutions. If she was disappointed, there is not a shred of evidence in her report to the community: "I wish that all of the Sisters might . . . have been listening in on the various conversations and discussions. The delegates brought to it a most intelligent cooperation. They had at heart the welfare of the Center and of the Sisters they represented."[8]

If Mother Mary Joseph's expectations were indeed higher, she probably realized that it would take more time and more experience with a broader number of Sisters to develop that far-reaching a policy. Also, she might not have realized beforehand that in the Catholic Church women were not allowed to work for degrees in theology.[9] Nevertheless, in these rapidly changing times her effort of 1929 continues to serve as a stimulus to strengthen the Maryknoll Sisters' theological preparation for mission on an ongoing basis. In the meantime, in 1931, with practical matters expedited, Mother Mary Joseph hoped the Sisters would ease more confidently into their mission land, now that they had "Constitutions they could claim as their very own."[10]

Mother Mary Joseph did not rely solely on policy statements to prepare the Sisters for mission. She gave regular conferences to encourage them and also to name the challenges they would confront. By 1944 the maturity of her assessment was sweeping in its breadth:

> You have the task of teaching by word and example the truths that others would avoid, of restoring and building up the faith that has been lost or weakened, of promoting unity among God's people, of sowing peace where there is discord and courage where there is weakness or fear. This calls for continuous sacrifice, for greatheartedness, for tireless striving against great odds.[11]

Ever realistic in her expectations, she was well aware that becoming a missioner is a lifetime process. From her first mission visitation in China she had undoubtedly seen that, as in her own life, the most crucial learning for the Sisters would come from the people themselves, those among whom they lived and worked. Her own formation for mission had emerged as the response of a woman who was very sensitive to her experiences in life. She urged the Sisters to be open and alert to their experiences and to profit by them.

Just as effectively as in her policies and conferences, Mother Mary Joseph shaped the missionary attitudes of the Sisters through her bold initiatives. Like the other Teresians, she had come to Hawthorne with no preconceived notions about religious life beyond the fact that it was a life given unreservedly for others. Mother Mary Joseph therefore gave free range to her vision of what religious life could be. She consistently encouraged the Sisters to develop their God-given personalities, to cultivate the raw material of their natural dispositions, but also to remain deeply attuned to the common good.

From the very beginning the Maryknoll women had expressed the determination to be Sisters who could adapt to all kinds of situations and cultures. Unwittingly, Mother Mary Joseph herself was the source of an idea that would indelibly stamp the congregation's mission thrust in China. During her first visitation in 1923 Father Francis X. Ford had noticed how easy it was for the Chinese women to approach her. Based on his observations, he developed a whole new approach for the Sisters' apostolate. Like the priests, they were to go from village to village, house to house, accept hospitality, eating what was put before them, sometimes for weeks on end, sacrificing all to manifest the mutuality of gospel living. It is no wonder that this apostolic style was awarded pride of place in Mother Mary Joseph's Mission Policy of 1929.

The early women were assuredly inspired when they identified adaptability as one of the most important traits for their lives. For them, the "field afar" was still on the far-distant horizon. They could not have realized yet the extent to which their well-being would depend on the kind of resilience to which they aspired. By 1930 Mother Mary Joseph could spell it out. "Adaptability," she said, "is that power of creating any where that we may be sent the feeling of fitting in, and of attempting anything which we are asked to do."[12] The Sisters in China had already had a lesson on adaptability when Ford's first effort to involve them in the direct apostolate had to be put on hold, almost before it got started, because of widespread unrest in the country. The method was resumed, however, and fully implemented in 1935 in the Kaying Prefecture of which Ford would become bishop within the year. Mother Mary Joseph's unqualified blessing on the venture is documented in her letter to Ford: "I am anxious to give you the full number of Sisters you desire; for, this particular phase of work has always been dearest to my heart. I believe it is our essential mission-ary work, along with the training of native Sisters."[13]

For the sake of mission Mother Mary Joseph took resolute steps, heedless of the risks of failure or censure. However, both she and Ford were happy to receive the spontaneous approval of Cardinal Fumasoni-Biondi, prefect of the Sacred Congregation for the Propagation of the Faith in Rome:

> I am aware of the courage and devotion which many Maryknoll Sisters have displayed . . . particularly in the vicariate of Kaying, where they have gone from house to house among the people and they have proven valuable helpers to the Fathers in reaching the non-Christians. Let us hope that this work may grow and that God may bless it, with abundant fruit.[14]

Ford was jubilant:

> Rome has gone out of its way to orientate the work of the Maryknoll Sisters, differentiating it from work hitherto considered the province of Sisters. . . . In short, Rome sets its approval on our thesis that foreign women can be missioners, just as foreign men can; or rather, it can be interpreted even more strongly as affirming that our Sisters should be direct missioners.[15]

Mother Mary Joseph, too, was elated. She believed so totally in the timeliness of Ford's method that it had not occurred to her to wait for approval to prepare more young Sisters for assignment to this apostolate in China. Many years later it is gratifying to note the ap-proving eye Anthony de Mello cast on her forthright style:

> I like what they said about the foundress of the Maryknoll Sisters: "She was a woman who had a cool head, a warm heart, and a sense of humor." That is what we need: a warm heart, ready to go all out with total generosity and greatheartedness; a cool head to be used for calculating how much we can do; and then a sense of humor.[16]

Like her spiritual mentor St. Teresa of Avila, Mother Mary Joseph was as "down to earth" as she was sublime in her molding of the con-gregation. Our mission, she said, is "to do the reaching out . . . and not wait for [people] to search for us," insisting on "the ready smile, the affable greeting, the radiating charm."[17] Yes, Maryknoll Sisters were to be attractive so that non-Christians might be drawn to them. Otherwise, "the [people] might easily reject the Christ who was an unknown to them."[18] That the Sisters could not risk. As she grew in her understanding of mission, so did her sense of awe at the sacredness and urgency of the task increase.

The story of a moment during her first visitation to China when she was particularly struck by the gracious gift of the mission vocation provides a most fitting description of her sense of mission. She was traveling to Ningpo, where the Charity Sisters had a thriving mission under the leadership of Sister Xavier Berkeley. Mother Mary Joseph explains that Ningpo was part of the Teresians' first lessons on foreign missions and that Sister Xavier was a household name for them.[19] She would not have dreamed of bypassing Ningpo, an overnight trip from Shanghai. The ship docked in the early morning of September 15 and the travelers got into rickshaws.[20] Mother Mary Joseph narrates:

> My coolie decided to take a different route from the others . . . going in and out of alleys that seemed to have no ending. . . . At the bridge, I did not know which way to turn so, dismissing the coolie I sat on the bridge knowing the others would follow . . . and fell to dreaming of God and His ways with men—the vast unbelieving hordes about me and the few scattered groups of valiant men and women who were giving their all to bring about the accomplishment of His will on earth. A tap on the shoulder—back to earth—and there beside me was a smiling coolie.[21]

The Sisters hastening toward her were distressed because the "Mère Générale" was sitting on that bridge alone. "And I," Mother Mary Joseph continues, "if I had wished to try, could never have made them understand how sweet were those moments of communion with my Lord—in the rosy freshness of the day—alone on a little bridge in China!"[22] Awed at finding herself in the midst of another culture, she was momentarily transported by God's all-encompassing love for the "vast unbelieving hordes" surrounding her and the part missioners were privileged to play in God's grand scheme of things. During her lifetime Mother Mary Joseph gave many conferences and retreats to the Sisters in which she consistently revealed her awe at God's presence in her life. The spirituality of this amazing woman was a gift not only for Maryknoll missioners in the first part of the twentieth century but for our time and for the world.

Part III

The Spirituality of
Mother Mary Joseph Rogers

14

The Presence of God

Mother Mary Joseph lived her entire life before Vatican II. When she died in 1955, Pius XII was pontiff; no one had ever heard of Angelo Roncalli, who became John XXIII; and no one had a clue that there was going to be a Second Vatican Council.

Mother Mary Joseph never pretended to be erudite, especially in spiritual matters. She was well educated for her time, having earned a bachelor of arts degree from Smith College in June 1905, but formal theology or scripture classes were not part of a secular education. To nourish her soul, she was blessed with a warm home life, regular church activities, the catechism classes of her youth, and the gift of an inquiring mind. Once she came to Maryknoll, the practice of daily prayer, regular spiritual conferences, and meditation on the scriptures enlarged her spirit. Everything at Maryknoll was oriented toward the foreign missions. When the time came for her to assume responsibility for the formation of women religious missioners, it was evident she had thrived in the atmosphere of Maryknoll's early days.

The Maryknoll Sisters' founder had learned to listen humbly to God's voice. In the opening conference of the community retreat she gave in 1931, she was disarmingly modest: "Let us attend the conferences, simple as they are, unlearned as they are; just little talks from my heart to yours."[1] She communicated simplicity at its best, as in the following year when she counseled the first-year novices to strive for perfection, impressing on them that they were to begin immediately because "for all of us, perfection really consists in doing to the very best of our ability, for the love of God, the duty of the moment. . . . Perfection, sanctity, holiness lies in the present moment, not in the years to come."[2]

Mother Mary Joseph seldom averts to her sources, except for St. Teresa of Avila, of whom she speaks as a companion and guide.[3] As she came to know the saint, she took note of St. Teresa's constant comings and goings in her work of reforming the Carmelites. "Such journeyings" she said, "would have been useless had she not borne with her the rich fruits of a close union with God."[4] She claimed that the saint's example showed the women in the early days how to make their busy lives fruitful: "Faithfulness to meditation and prayer, trying constantly to be mindful of God's presence in our souls—these were the foundation of our missionary life."[5]

Like Teresa, Mother Mary Joseph was so adept and consistent in identifying the "really real" that it seems to have been innate to her nature, she who was endowed with an abundance of common sense. What was "most real" to her was God's unimaginable immediacy to each person. This conviction, expressed throughout her conferences as "the presence of God," is now recognized by the Maryknoll Sisters as the taproot in her mentoring of the community.

Mother Mary Joseph never tired of telling the Sisters, "We should always try to live in the presence of God."[6] While only two of her conferences are titled "Presence of God," the expression virtually punctuates all of her talks. A 1921 letter to the Sisters on the West Coast and China urges them to cultivate the presence of God. *Cultivate,* one of her signature words, occurs often and in a variety of contexts. The Sisters were to cultivate everything, from a warm smile to the love of God and mutual charity. The word itself is engaging. One has to work at cultivation, exert some energy, if one is to reap the gardener's delight in the promise of a good harvest, and this is equally so for the cultivation of virtue.

Just as it is not always easy to produce good fruit, as time went on it was not always easy for Mother Mary Joseph to communicate how the Sisters might understand the practice of the presence of God. In 1947, she spoke of the difficulties she had encountered in her ongoing efforts to inculcate the practice among the Sisters.

> In the early days (we didn't know much of these things—we don't know much more now) when I'd tell the Sisters that we should try to be always in the presence of God, some of them said this was impossible. How could one do one's work and be thinking of God at the same time? But, if someone we love is in great sorrow or experiencing a great joy—or—just someone we love to whom nothing in particular is happening at the moment—we will have that person in the back of our minds and continually—as soon as our thoughts are freed from the task in hand—they will fly to that person.[7]

In 1929, much earlier in the life of the congregation, she had addressed the Sisters' objections when she introduced the cultivation of the contemplative spirit as one of the congregation's great works.[8] The following year she added: "So it is with the presence of God in our souls. We go about our work: we do it well . . . Christ . . . in the background of our minds, ever ready to take full possession of us when free moments come. . . . Just as easily as conversation with another Sister with whom we live."[9] "And that," she concluded, in a retreat ten years later, "is all we mean by habitual recollection. It is very possible! It ought to characterize every Maryknoll Sister."[10] Mother Mary Joseph obviously continued to mull over the objections she encountered until she was satisfied with the clarity with which she could positively affirm the possibility of habitual recollection as "the one thing necessary" (Lk 10:40).

Although it would be reason enough to strive to remain in the presence of God based simply on God's total involvement with us, Mother Mary Joseph adds a practical reason, based on the experiences from her first mission visitation, which were still very fresh in her mind. "This communing with God is especially important to us as missioners," she said in her 1930 retreat:

> Just as you have been surprised at finding the difficulties that you anticipated in your religious life greatly diminished, just so are you going to find the difficulties that you anticipated in the mission field far from your anticipation. It won't be the climate, hard beds, food, but loneliness. If you have not cultivated the habit of speaking with Christ, you will find yourself frightened and alone in a great desert. So learn to listen to him. There is no need for us to feel discouraged because God is with us.[11]

God's abiding presence was hardly newfound faith on her part, she who had asserted in her letter of 1921, "God never abandons us."[12] The experience of appalling loneliness, however, *that* was new, and it became a constant refrain in her conferences, providing ever more reason to cultivate the presence of God.

While her words are addressed directly to the Sisters and the circumstances they would find in the missions, no one is a stranger to the devastating effects of loneliness, so prevalent in our modern society, particularly among immigrants, the chronically ill, the elderly—the orphan and the widow, in biblical terms. Mother Mary Joseph reiterates many times that the presence of God is the underlying reason for everything any person does. As early as 1929, in the second of her two conferences that year on the presence of God,[13] she said:

> One of the strong defenses against letting things that are opposed to God into our heart is the practice of the presence of God. We

know that God is everywhere: mountain tops, depths of the earth and sea. God is in us and the marvel of it all is that we realize it so little. If we did realize it we would be overwhelmed. We should be forced to lie prostrate in Adoration of the Godhead dwelling within us.[14] Unfortunately, however, we go to the other extreme and we go about from day to day as though God were not with us.[15]

How did Mother Mary Joseph expect the Sisters to cultivate the presence of God so that "their hearts would be filled with constant longing for union with God?"[16] She made several practical suggestions. One was the custom of saying very short ejaculatory prayers as, for example, a plea for God's mercy, or what may be more familiar to many people, the repetition of a mantra as in centering prayer, the purpose of which is to raise one's mind and heart to God intentionally: "In our active life, we do not have time for sustained long prayer, but when we are going back and forth from our work, how simple it is for us to keep united to God and to make us conscious of [God's] presence in our souls."[17]

To guard against compulsiveness in prayer, Mother Mary Joseph wanted the Sisters to understand that "of ourselves we can do nothing to insure our salvation. We also know that with the grace of God we can do all things."[18]

So that the Sisters would never be far from the conscious presence of Christ, her letter of 1921 holds a second suggestion, "It would be well to form the habit not only of every morning, offering the thoughts words and acts of the day to God, but to repeat that offering frequently during the day . . . to ensure what is absolutely essential."[19] This calls to mind St. Paul's reminder in his letter to the Colossians, which Mother Mary Joseph quoted to strengthen her point: "All whatsoever you do in word or in work, do all in the name of the Lord Jesus Christ . . . whatsoever you do, do it from the heart" (Col 3:17, 23).

> And if we do all for love of God, direct our intentions well, and consciously live in God's presence, we shall find that our day's acts show forth the other characteristics desired, zeal, devotedness, love for the sublime work to which we have been called, and we shall find nothing too hard, no sacrifice too great in the performance of our daily duties.[20]

A third practice that Mother Mary Joseph advocated as early as 1926 was the practice of the Particular Examen, saying that it "is practically indispensable if one hopes to advance in holiness, or to overcome one's faults, or to acquire any particular virtue."[21] The point of it, she hastened to explain, was "to gain the spirit of recollection, the practice of the presence of God."[22] And so to be conscious of God's abiding presence rather than examine oneself on one's sinfulness all the time, it is just as helpful to focus on a particular virtue one would like to acquire.

Each of these practices, Mother Mary Joseph insists, is helpful, "not only to give intelligent loving direction to a day but you will notice a marked increase in your consciousness of God's dear presence."[23] Long before the Examen of Conscience metamorphosed into the Examen of Consciousness,[24] Mother Mary Joseph had understood its underlying value.

With reference to prayer and the practice of the presence of God, the obviously helpful aspect that Mother Mary Joseph does not mention is the need for silence. She did not need to mention it because during her lifetime silence was a structured part of apostolic religious life. Sisters were careful to maintain a respectful silence and quiet throughout the day and throughout the house, especially in the workplace. They understood the value and the need for silence, not only to focus on their work, but also to foster the spirit of recollection.

While the days of active religious are no longer circumscribed by silence, an atmosphere of recollection is undeniably advantageous, especially in view of Mother Mary Joseph's prompting in 1931, for the sake of mission: "Sisters in active mission life ought to feel drawn to cultivate in themselves a very deep consciousness of the presence of God. By carrying God's presence within them, they will present a beautiful picture of God . . . people will see God in them."[25]

When Mother Mary Joseph enjoined the delegates at the General Chapter of 1946 to practice the presence of God, she was offering them the fruit of her lifelong meditation. For her, the practice was akin to single-mindedness, transparency, and congruence in one's life:

> There is no room for complexity in our dealings, for mixed motives, for doing other than the truth. "Behold I come to do thy will" (Heb 10:7), and "I have naught else but Christ and him crucified" (1 Cor 2:2). A missionary Sister must deliver a message and it must be clear and ungarbled and consistent with her own living. . . . A missionary Sister, above all others, must correspond in speech and life; she often is the first to breathe the name of God by which Name alone comes salvation; she often is the only Christ to pass through pagan villages and her soul must magnify the Lord as she bears his honor and reputation in her keeping. A wrong note and her message is

distorted, a false step and she leads away from Christ, a pose or studied attitude and she twists the image of Christ.[26]

Fifteen years earlier, in a meditation to the whole community, Mother Mary Joseph mused that if the Sisters were conscious of the presence of God on a continual basis, "there would be an end of criticisms, unkindness, uncharitableness, and if there were an end to all these things, we would have the beginning of paradise here on earth."[27]

Later, in an address to superiors, she raises up the benefits of the presence of God in such a way that the Sisters would never forget: "Conscious of [God's] presence, our humility will deepen, our charity towards one another will glow more warmly, our religious obligations will take on a new flavor, and we will find all things working together for good. For God is love, and where love is there is God—there is peace."[28]

As far back as 1929 Mother Mary Joseph had sensed that some Sisters seemed discouraged by their inattention to the presence of God in their lives, at having "lost" so many years. She addresses them tenderly:

So much of our life has already passed. We know not what is before us. I am sure that all of us look back with real grief at the time wasted, opportunities lost of cultivating that consciousness of the presence of Christ in our souls. If we have advanced somewhat along the way of this practice, let us thank God and persevere. If up to the present, it has meant little in our lives, let us not go along blindly and struggling without it. Let us begin in a very simple, loving way to remind ourselves of it.[29]

Giving up in discouragement was not part of Mother Mary Joseph's spirituality! She constantly reminded the Sisters not to lose heart. Like St. Teresa, they needed to be willing to start over again and again, because with God there is no time, nothing is ever "lost."

In sum, although Mother Mary Joseph had not studied theology per se, her grasp of God's "unimaginable immediacy" places her among God's friends and prophets. The presence of God was the taproot, the underlying reason for everything she did and enjoined on the Sisters. To that end she offered them several practical ways to cultivate habitual recollection. Awareness of God's presence not only wards off the crushing loneliness she witnessed in the lives of missioners, but it also shapes them in virtues essential for mission: single-mindedness, transparency, and congruence.

15

Contemplation and Action

There are several binary oppositions in Mother Mary Joseph's writings, including contemplation and action.[1] Binary oppositions are apparent contradictions that if held in creative tension generate tremendous energy for the revitalization of a group or a community. Generally, people have a tendency to favor one over the other within the pair. This tends to be destructive of the person and also disrupts "the social harmony, development and transformation of the group."[2] Keeping the balance requires attention and effort on the part of the individual.

In 1994 Maryknoll Sister Barbara Hendricks, in a conversation with Gerald Arbuckle, a cultural anthropologist, learned that the charism of the founder contains the binary oppositions that are characteristic of a particular spirit.[3] She then proceeded to identify five binary oppositions in Mother Mary Joseph's writings: contemplation and action, joy and suffering, individuality and common good, fearless honesty and compassion, and unity of spirit and diversity of gifts.[4] These elements, which affect the life and mission of every Maryknoll Sister, are Mother Mary Joseph's gift to her community, although she knew how difficult it would be to keep the balance.

Contemplation and action, unity and diversity, and individuality and common good are treated in this chapter and the two chapters that follow. The fearless honesty and compassion binary is incorporated within Chapter 19. The fifth, joy and suffering, runs as a thread throughout Mother Mary Joseph's conferences and does not emerge as a distinct topic in her writings. It bears mention, however, because she missed no opportunity to remind the Sisters to "cultivate the habit of being happy under adverse conditions and despite sufferings. It is no grace to bear sufferings with a long face, to mope about it, to pour forth the tale of our difficulties to every passerby. We are all so prone to do this."[5] Mother Mary Joseph saw how neglect of the balance between joy and suffering could sap the energy of a group.

Mother Mary Joseph has no conference in her collection entitled "Contemplation and Action," nor is it noted anywhere that she was familiar with the designation of binary opposition. Yet, throughout her writings Mother Mary Joseph affirms the equal indispensability of contemplation and action. This conviction came by way of St. Teresa of Avila, that splendid sixteenth-century Carmelite contemplative, who, according to Mother Mary Joseph, was one of the strongest influences in the development of the spiritual life of the community.[6] "Our small group was still floundering along the little known ways of the spiritual life," when Father James Anthony Walsh held her up as a model and patron, a choice that she claimed was anything but haphazard on his part.[7]

> He knew well that whatever our religious status might be, we, a little group of clerical and household workers—bound to a life of increasing activity—would come to be a useless body if our tasks were not properly motivated, and our hearts and minds oriented to God. . . . Though a contemplative Teresa combined that life with a most active one, and in spite of incredible preoccupations, kept her heart and mind centered in God.[8]

Even beyond St. Teresa's influence on the lifestyle of the women, Mother Mary Joseph credited her for leading the Maryknoll Sisters to the Dominican Family "with its wealth of spiritual treasures, that perfect balance of the contemplative and active life which our [particular] life requires, opportunity for our personal sanctification, for intensive prayer for Maryknoll and the missions, and for carrying on the ever increasing work resulting from the miraculous growth of the Society."[9] In a much later conference to the Maryknoll Sisters, she said,

> I always find it pleasant to recall that little incident in St. Teresa's life when, before Mass, she [had a vision of] St. Dominic (1170–1221) in his chapel in the Church of Santa Cruz. There he promised to aid her in all her enterprises. . . . I like to think that perhaps St. Teresa, in gratitude for all St. Dominic did for her, gave us to him to be nurtured in his great, loving, apostolic heart.[10]

In that first decade (1912–20), even as the women yearned for stability through religious life, they were otherwise exclusively concerned with the well-being of the Catholic Foreign Mission Society of America. Mother Mary Joseph explains that "the probability of actual mission work for us was so remote as to be little more than a dream."[11]

In 1948 she told the community: "That any of us would ever see the actual mission field was a very remote prospect in Father Walsh's mind. Some day perhaps the goal would be reached, but not in our time."[12] In that first decade the women took heart in the tradition "that St. Teresa had gained by prayer as many conversions as had Xavier through preaching."[13]

Despite the restrictive limitations foreseen for the women in those early years, it was an endless source of amazement for Mother Mary Joseph that the community was established on the solid spiritual foundation of the Dominican charism of contemplation and action. She saw more and more clearly as the years passed that holding the graced tension between contemplation and action would make all the difference for the young missionary Sisters:

> Our life was a busy, distracted one, each day too short to see its tasks completed. We soon learned that a missioner must be a contemplative in action; that our hearts must be on fire with love of God and souls. Meditation, faithfulness to times of prayer and trying to be constantly mindful of God's presence in our souls were the foundation of this missionary life we had chosen to follow, a life so busy that we often wondered—as we do even today—how we could live at once a life of prayer and a life of extreme activity. . . . This laid the foundation for our Dominican life which combines perfectly the ways of prayer and activity.[14]

From the foregoing and from all her writings, Mother Mary Joseph manifestly thrived in the Dominican charism, and she constantly enjoined the Sisters to claim it as their heritage.[15]

Sometimes Mother Mary Joseph's expression is "contemplative *and* active," but most often she speaks of "contemplatives *in* action." There may be a subtle distinction between *and* and *in*: *and* seems to convey more clearly that both contemplation and action must be held in tension. However, it was the apparent contradiction between the two lifestyles that created resistance in some community members. Not all the Sisters were convinced.

Some Sisters understood that their prayer should inform their work, but how were they to be contemplatives *and* active Sisters? They contended that the two lifestyles could not be combined, that they were "diametrically opposed."[16] It was the same problem the Sisters had with staying in the presence of God while working. And when Mother Mary Joseph proposed sung vespers, for some it was the "last straw."[17] Even with the distance of time, their murmurings are almost audible:

"We are more contemplative than active; we are attempting too much." Her inclusion of these comments in her conference shows how graciously Mother Mary Joseph acknowledged the Sisters' misgivings. She invited their comments, preferring by far to deal with outright opposition than undercover rumblings: "The Sisters who feel this are quite within their right when they say so—and all of us should be honest in our consideration of this [matter]."[18] She too was concerned about overburdening the community "and more particularly those who will come after us, with spiritual exercises that will become distasteful and crushing."[19]

She dealt with these objections compassionately, but, as was her wont, she was quick to name the essentials that needed to be held in disciplined tension:

> We must bear in mind the necessity of enriching our lives, for we cannot give to others what we do not possess. . . . I try not to over-emphasize spiritualities or to burden our Sisters. I believe, however, that in this age there is more danger of worldliness creeping in than of over-stressing the religious end of our daily lives. We live in a period of worldliness, of super-activity, of love and interest in our material well-being to the exclusion of anything that interferes with it.[20]

The term *comfort zones* had not yet been coined in 1944, yet Mother Mary Joseph aptly described them.

It is fair to speculate on how Mother Mary Joseph herself understood the way in which contemplation and action could be combined. Nowhere is it clearer than in the talk she gave to the 1937 General Chapter Delegates at the Maryknoll Cloister.

> I never go back on the ideal and the idea that every Maryknoll Sister is a contemplative. . . . When I say "contemplative," I do not mean in the sense of one set apart to dwell upon the things of God. I mean that we must be so trained, have so formed our affections . . . our inward gaze fixed solely upon [God], and no matter what distractions, no matter what works, what trials, sickness, separation caused by death—always our first thought, our involuntary action, even, is to accept everything with our eyes fixed upon the face of Christ.[21]

She was straight as an arrow in maintaining that it was never a question of one or the other, but both/and. In an earlier meditation on

St. Dominic she had specified that "the ideal of our vocation is to work and to work hard, then to go before Our Lord for refreshment and rest. Labor, the active life; prayer, the contemplative. Both blend perfectly; one is never prejudiced against the other."[22]

Earlier still, after the General Chapter in 1931, in her report to the community at Maryknoll, she wrote:

> We have been called to that union of the contemplative with the active. Few of us are conscious of it. We know that in our souls is the desire to go to the ends of the earth to save souls. Where we find failure it is because self has been predominant, because Christ has not dwelt with us. It must be our constant effort, our constant work to have that perfect blending of the contemplative with the active.[23]

Mother Mary Joseph did more than simply exhort the Sisters. Late in November of 1943 she also named the key challenge with her characteristic fearless honesty: "Unfortunately, many of us work hard—but pray little—we lose sight of God, relying wholly upon ourselves."[24] Maryknoll Sisters were to be like John the Baptist, she continued, opening the way for Christ to enter the hearts of people, persuading them by the example of their humility.

Eleven days later, in her conference for the New Year, she expanded on why the balance between prayer and action was so critical for Maryknoll Sisters. Without prayer, the Sisters would become listless and "an apathetic worker anywhere . . . pulls down the morale of others and weakens our whole well-being."[25]

On the recollection day of 1944 Mother Mary Joseph returned to many of the ideas she had propounded in 1937.

> We have undertaken a most active, strenuous, wearing form of religious life—that of an apostle—and we find no day is ever long enough for all the things we would crowd into it. This life must at the same time be deeply, intensely spiritual. Like St. Francis Xavier, we are to be contemplatives in action if we are to be successful in our apostolate.[26]

Much earlier, in 1929, she wrote:

> St. Dominic created a new order, blending the ideals of the old life with the needs of the new. He never lost sight of the fact that . . . without personal sanctity nothing could be done for the saving of others. . . . No longer would the religious remain within the convent

walls, expecting the world to come to them. . . . So we find ourselves today in an order which has for its ideal the mingling of the active and the contemplative life. It was the life of Christ Himself. . . . He spent years in preparation for His short ministry . . . doing good, healing the sick, blind, lame, raising the dead, driving out devils, and yet He was always the fullest expression of Divine Charity. Here then is the Model for us. Ours is an active life . . . and yet if it is not a contemplative one also our toilings are going to be in vain. . . . To cultivate this contemplative spirit in our own soul is one of our great works.[27]

Mother Mary Joseph's vision was incisive. She wanted the Maryknoll Sisters to be holy women whose intense active life was faithfully informed by prayer.

In sum, while Mother Mary Joseph never titled a conference "Contemplation and Action," this topic is clearly dear to her heart. She took every opportunity to call the Sisters' attention to what she saw as indispensable for a missionary Sister. That this feature should come to the community through the agency of Teresa of Avila simply confirmed for Mother Mary Joseph the gracious guidance of God in the formation of her beloved community. For some Sisters, however, it was contemplative or active, not both. Mother Mary Joseph listened to their misgivings, and how fortunate for the community that she sought to clarify rather than go back on her understanding of this apparent contradiction. As very active missioners the Sisters needed to cultivate that special quality of affective presence in the world, one rooted in their intimacy with God because, in so many ways, Mother Mary Joseph insisted, "we cannot give what we do not have."

16

Unity of Spirit
and Diversity of Gifts

When Mother Mary Joseph speaks about diversity in her conferences, her predominant concern is with the differences that arise from the various backgrounds of the Sisters. Intercultural issues on diversity had not yet surfaced and were not part of her experience, even in 1955 when she died. Yet, Sisters from Asian cultures had entered the Maryknoll Sisters' community almost from the beginning. On her second mission visitation in China in the late 1920s, Mother Mary Joseph returned to Maryknoll accompanied by a Chinese woman who became Sister Maria Teresa, the first of many Maryknoll Sisters to come from Asia. When Maria Teresa entered, she was simply assimilated into the American congregation.

Although the Maryknoll Sisters believed in building up the local church, they prided themselves on being open to receiving women of other cultures into their congregation. Eventually, young women in several mission countries expressed a desire to become Maryknoll Sisters. They entered a community that was very happy to receive them, but one that did not anticipate the hidden dimensions of rubbing elbows in community across cultures. The increased presence of Sisters from a variety of cultures was an unexpected blessing—and also a challenge for everyone as assumptions came under scrutiny.

By the 1978 General Assembly the Sisters had made the conscious turn from assimilation to integration. They had learned that when a new candidate enters, regardless of her culture, everybody has to change, to adapt, not only the new person. Ideally, everybody moves over to make a welcoming space. Life in community necessitates doing this over and over again, regardless of cultural differences.

This kind of learning asserted itself over time until it led the Sisters to recognize racism in themselves. The awareness of the possibility of being tinged with racism grew very slowly, emerging as a viable topic

89

only at the 1990 General Assembly. At that point some Sisters, especially the North Americans, still adamantly denied that they were racist. Racism was something "out there," a problem in society mainly perpetrated by bigots. However, workshops and discussions on racism eventually opened their eyes to the disparity between their Christian life and their assumptions. The Sisters began to recognize the superiority they unconsciously conveyed through their behavior and their words.[1] This new self-knowledge brought freedom opening them to grace upon grace.

Since the foregoing intercultural issues had not yet surfaced during Mother Mary Joseph's lifetime, it should not come as a surprise that they are not treated in her conferences. The differences on which she concentrated, for the most part, were based on individual dispositions, as in her talk in 1930:

> Sometimes as I look over the community and doubtless you yourselves have done the same, and see our Sisters from all parts of the country, from all stations in life, with different heritages from their parents, and utterly different dispositions working in harmony and peace, I marvel, and then I adore God for his immeasurable graces given to us.[2]

It is interesting to note that, with only a slight adjustment, what she said in 1930 is as relevant now as it was then and as immediately applicable for intercultural understanding:

> Sometimes as I look over the community and doubtless you yourselves have done the same, and see our Sisters from all parts of the *world*, from all stations in life, with different *languages and heritages* from their parents, and utterly different dispositions working in harmony and peace, I marvel, and then I adore God for his immeasurable graces given to us.

Had Mother Mary Joseph lived long enough to experience the blessings and challenges of the "blending of nations" within the Maryknoll Sisters' Congregation, she would not have had to change her statement in any way. It was her hope that the Sisters would live together in unity. Most basic of all, however, she understood that living in peace and harmony was not of the Sisters' own doing: "How blessed are we who live in a religious community in which God is the motive power, the directive power, the source and the object of our love. If it were not for this, do you think for one moment that we could live together in harmony and peace? We know that we could not."[3]

Charity, the sure foundation of unity, did not always come naturally. Mother Mary Joseph knew that. She knew that coming "from different homes, different surroundings and different experiences" puts its own peculiar strain on community, as she illustrates in Advent of 1931:

> It is only natural that we find some Sisters we like and some we don't. . . . I don't ask you to love one another alike—no, that is impossible [because] God did not make us that way. And I don't ask you not to be conscious of the defects others have in their dispositions which make it hard to bear with them. I don't expect you to be blind; after all, we are intelligent.[4]

To the Sisters in the Cloister, which had just been established and where they were so few initially, she spoke of how they could expect their life to be different in that they would "rub elbows constantly." Most of the Sisters had only lived at the Motherhouse, where it was possible to live peaceably with a wide variety of temperaments. But in the Cloister the Sisters would soon experience that "we are not bound together by ties of natural affection," as was also certainly true for the Sisters who were living in groups of two, three, or four in China at the time.[5]

If not with natural affection, how then were they bound? According to Mother Mary Joseph, "In looking at your Sisters, you must see them as they are in the eyes of God. Everyone has lovable traits. Sometimes we have to hunt around to find such traits but they are there, and a little interest and kindness will bring them out. Oftentimes, you will find something very nice."[6]

Over the years she emphasized this instruction—that the Sisters see one another as God sees them—reminding them that they were "inclined to forget that, like ourselves, our Sisters are made to the image and likeness of God."[7]

By then she was well aware of her Sisters' prowess in mission. She had seen firsthand what they could do, and it was beyond her wildest imagining. She made use of that too in her 1941 Christmas message in order to draw their attention to what might be even more demanding than doing great things in mission: "Our charity is the index of our love of God and souls. What we fail to give our Sisters, we shall fail to give to thirsting souls outside."[8]

Three weeks later, in January 1942, she expanded on this notion:

> We think we would spend ourselves totally "feeding the sheep" in our missions, but there are other sheep. We are in the midst of them

day and night. We work with them, eat with them, sit . . . beside them at table, pray with them. We have the same obligation of feeding one another, of loving one another, of enlightening one another, of keeping close to one another, drawing one another from danger in the safety and security of the love which envelops and enfolds our entire [religious] family.[9]

In that same talk Mother Mary Joseph identifies the various ways in which the unity of the community is weakened when some Sisters act as if they are superior to others, while others become discouraged and feel they are of no use to the community. She also saw some begin to show little concern for the community, choosing to live "their own little life apart by themselves."[10]

Mother Mary Joseph then appeals to each Sister to take to heart that "nothing is more momentous than that our life as a community should be kept intact and vigorous; idealistic, as well as realistic."[11] In her closing remarks, she specifically enjoins the Sisters to

ask for an increase of understanding of what unity means, of the sacrifices it demands of us, of the efforts it calls upon us to make. Let us ask especially for the love which must animate our hearts if we are to work for one another, to sacrifice for one another—and all because we love Christ and would do nothing that would rend his seamless robe, as expressed in the unity of the Church and in the unity which must exist among us.[12]

Regarding life in community, the Sisters could expect some very practical advice from Mother Mary Joseph.

If someone tells you another Sister is very nice, say "yes," and don't go fishing up something you have heard about her that is not nice. When you know that a Sister admires another Sister, do all you can to increase her admiration and don't allow yourself to become one of those critics who is always going about breaking down idols.[13]

In the context of a retreat, Mother Mary Joseph gave one conference on charity and another on jealousy. In them, she appeals to the best that is in the Sisters.

Charity: Let us learn to love the success of one another. If I get something more than you get, rejoice with me, and if you receive greater praise or if you are more successful in your work than I am in mine, then I beg God to let me rejoice with you and never to envy you but to feel that whatever comes to each one of you is just as much mine as any success or blessings which come to me, because we are all part of one family, all working for the same end, and all animated with the love of the same God. This should be our attitude towards one another, and just as we rejoice with one another in our good fortune, let us sorrow with one another when grief comes and disappointment and failure; let us make that sorrow as truly our own as if we ourselves were suffering directly under that misfortune. These are two practical manifestations of love without which we cannot expect to be pleasing to God.[14]

Jealousy: I find so often that when I speak with praise of the talents of one Sister to another, perhaps of her disposition, or her virtue, almost invariably there is someone ready to lessen the honor that is being paid to her, by some such remark as: "Well, if you knew her better, you wouldn't say that." They cannot bear to hear another Sister praised. They haven't the largeness of heart to be proud of the talents of their Sisters in religion.[15]

In her concern about the wholesomeness of community life, Mother Mary Joseph spoke of instances when a single Sister can spoil the harmony of a whole house: "We should be kind and tolerant to a sister who has a mean and whiney [sic] disposition, but if it is chronic, we should cure her of it."[16] She does not suggest how this cure might be affected, but she apparently recognizes that some people resist being cured. She adds:

Such people should be gotten out of the community before final vows. When this had not been done, unfortunately, then the Sisters should make up their minds to let that sister alone[17] . . . for the spirit of the house should not be spoiled by a morose individual. Our community is our home, the place where we should grow holy in sweetness and love of God, in loyalty to one another.[18]

What Mother Mary Joseph does not explicitly say in this conference is that each one has an obligation to work on her own rough edges. Elsewhere she says that it is never acceptable to claim, "This is the way I am." In one of her many talks to the delegates at the General Chapter in 1931 she comes very close to making that point: "Each one of us is potentially the one who can make others happy. We should strive against carelessness and selfishness, and try to do all that we can to make our companions happy, and therefore holier."[19] Her last line in this paragraph suggests how people can be "holier" if they are "happy": "Prevent others, my dear children, with the blessings of thy sweetness."[20]

Speaking on fraternal charity, Mother Mary Joseph quotes St. Teresa to make her point: "When opportunity occurs, take some burden upon yourself to ease your neighbor of it." She continues:

> As you know, I have often spoken to you about that. There is a great tendency in a life where people have much to do to say, "She has as much time to do her work as I have myself. These free moments are mine." There are very few days that go by when we cannot help one another. But balance it! There's nothing that tries one so much as to have people always forcing themselves upon you, making themselves so prominent that you can hardly breathe. Be careful in your attentions to one another that you do not make yourselves boresome.[21]

Mother Mary Joseph had been reading between the lines of some of the letters from the Sisters telling her about conditions they found difficult. The "conditions" they disclosed weighed on her heart, as is evident from her response:

> I have wished for some time to talk to you on a matter of growing concern to me. I refer to what *seems* to me a rather steady weakening of the bond of charity. I hope and feel that *seems* is the right word to use, for if there is an actual and really conscious lessening of mutual love in Christ, I shall indeed be heartsick and only the deepest confidence in the charity of Christ towards us will clarify my vision of our future usefulness as a religious body.[22]

Without the bond of charity there was no way and no reason that the congregation could or should continue.

Because charity is of the essence for community life, the matter of good relationships was a constant refrain in Mother Mary Joseph's writings. She called on St. Francis de Sales, who said, "Cultivate not only a solid, but a tender, gentle, meek love for those about you." And she repeats: "He says, 'Cultivate it.' He realizes that it doesn't come naturally."[23] She constantly reminded the Sisters to cultivate mutual charity and to practice it "until it becomes as natural to us as breathing. The religious house is not a business house; it is a craftshop, if we may call it by any name, in which one is striving to produce the most perfect thing that is possible in herself and others."[24]

No aspect of mutual charity escaped her attention. She enjoined the Sisters to cure anyone who persisted in "small gossipy talk. . . . I don't mean knock them down."[25] Once again, Mother Mary Joseph leaves the cure to the ingenuity of the Sisters, but in this case she offers a suggestion that she reiterates in several conferences. The Sisters might at least redirect the conversation, she says, by reversing the way they usually express themselves. For example, "Very often when someone says something good about a Sister, another retorts, "Yes, she's nice, but . . . ""[26] Rather than add to this negative way of thinking, she suggests that Sisters respond:

> Sister may be gloomy, may be silent, or afraid. [There is no need to deny it], but she has these lovely things about her, and name two or three. . . . It is just a little reversal, but oftentimes it is an opportunity to ward off contempt. Yet, we are not blind. Nobody says we must swallow a person wholesale. This is ridiculous hypocrisy.[27]

Mother Mary Joseph urged the Sisters to turn another's thoughts in the right direction. "Don't be afraid of being thought a 'goody-goody.' Recognize the difference between the person who is merely pious and the person who is trying to do the right thing, being kind and generous in everything."[28]

Always realistic, Mother Mary Joseph also says that when it comes to gossip, although "we can all think of somebody else who is guilty, we need to start with ourselves."[29]

Another issue that Mother Mary Joseph found distressing was that of Sisters discussing community matters with outsiders. On this point she expressed the hope of regaining "our family spirit which, in a way, has become diminished because [Sisters did not keep things to themselves]." Mother Mary Joseph had to be very circumspect about what she could say, and she felt bad about this. She gave it a second thought, however, and together with her council, she decided to try to resume talking more openly with the Sisters, leaving it up to them "to prove whether or not we can get back to [sharing freely]."[30]

Characteristically, Mother Mary Joseph was more prone to believe in the Sisters' capacity for maturity than to curtail her largeness of heart because of their weakness. She believed in them and was wont to urge them "as a protest against the lovelessness of the world to put your lovely charity into action by kind acts, encouraging words, prayers and the glad sharing of one another's joys and sorrows."[31] "Unless the whole spirit of charity fills our life we cannot have a happy life. . . . Make charity the great virtue of your lives. In a large community . . . we are apt to . . . get away from the feeling of looking out and reaching out to love everybody."[32]

Mother Mary Joseph insisted that love can never be measured. Although people are more inclined to be aware of those they know and love, they must have a heart for all, "even if we don't know them."[33]

In the twenty-first century Mother Mary Joseph's insistence on charity resounds in the hearts of the Sisters as they strive to be true to her vision, she who never faltered in her belief that "God has yet a great work for us to do; but the realization of this vision depends on you and me as individuals and on our cooperation. Do we love enough, do we work enough, do we pray enough, do we suffer enough? Maryknoll's future depends on our answer."[34]

The intercultural issues that have engaged the community, especially since the 1978 General Assembly, were not part of Mother Mary Joseph's experience. For her, diversity consisted in individuality, and she focused her attention on the unity that needed to be rooted in charity. She was characteristically realistic, and her common sense always prevailed as she called the Sisters to embrace the sacrifices entailed in living and working for one another on the path to holiness, "preventing one another by our sweetness." She urged them constantly: "You must see your Sisters as they are in the eyes of God."[35]

17

Individuality and Common Good

Up until the Second Vatican Council (1962–65), active religious life was monastically ordered. Days were thoroughly structured from the moment of rising to the time of retiring, and the schedule encompassed worship, prayer, meals, assigned work, recreation, housekeeping charges, and other duties such as serving and/or reading at meals, pantry and kitchen duty, and the like. There were long periods of silence, and many areas in the house were designated as places of strict silence. And, as was true for most religious communities, at Maryknoll the Sisters all looked alike, dressed in Maryknoll gray. However, at the same time, the Maryknoll Sisters were encouraged to develop their own individuality because Mother Mary Joseph did not want them cut from the same mold. At Maryknoll, despite appearances, there would be no two alike!

To this day every Maryknoll Sister takes pride in Mother Mary Joseph's uncommon vision for women religious, especially for her time. Although raised in a Catholic home, she did not attend parochial school, which may account for her remaining relatively untouched by the Catholic culture of the time. Thus, her vision of what religious life could be was shaped more by the resilience needed in foreign mission than by traditional expectations of religious. From the very first decade of Maryknoll (1912–20) she and the Teresians consciously chose to become Sister missioners who could adjust or adapt to all kinds of situations and cultures. They never could have foreseen the prodigious energy their choice released in the succeeding generations of Maryknoll Sisters as they, in turn, faced the challenges of stepping into the unknown.

Individuality was so dear to Mother Mary Joseph's heart that she spoke of it at every opportunity, especially in the context of the Maryknoll spirit.[1] Individuality did not arise by chance in the congregation of the Maryknoll Sisters. Mother Mary Joseph introduced it very deliberately, as she intimates in a 1940 conference, "We have tried from the beginning to cultivate a spirit which is extremely difficult and which for a long time might have been misunderstood even by those

97

nearest to us."[2] Her word "cultivate" suggests that this spirit does not spring up by itself and that it is not as easy as it seems. To launch and to sustain such a spirit requires ongoing effort.

She spoke about individuality at length in 1931:

> As I talk on retreat Sundays, I often stress the Maryknoll Spirit which we are striving to inculcate in our Sisters. It is a very difficult task, for we are trying to have the Sisters preserve their naturalness, to be open and frank, ready with their smile, to act as magnets drawing people to them, and not repel their little overtures of friendliness, and at the same time, not fail in religious dignity and modesty. We have tried to profit by the experience of other Orders in the matter of religious decorum in general, but we felt almost from the beginning that the nature of our work demanded something different from the generally accepted religious manner. We need winsomeness and magnetism to invite people to come to us.[3]

The previous year Mother Mary Joseph told the community that as Christ-bearers the Sisters would need all of their individuality, generosity, graciousness, sweetness, simplicity, and powers of gentle persuasiveness, in short, "all that the good God has given us."[4] The reason was clear. Unless non-Christians were attracted to the Sisters, they might easily reject the Christ who was an unknown to them.[5] *That*, the Sisters could not risk.

The case for individuality did not rest there. Mother Mary Joseph reiterated in many instances that the Sisters could misunderstand the whole meaning of individuality and affirmed that she was not suggesting in any way that the Sisters celebrate themselves. Individuality had nothing to do with the narcissism of individualism. Mother Mary Joseph stressed the challenge of the Sisters keeping their individuality while at the same time not settling to remain the way they were. It was imperative to cast out "what [was] objectionable in it, finding and using what [was] good and beautiful in it and supernaturalizing this, and then, using it not for ourselves, not for any honor or distinction . . . but only with the desire to promote God's honor and glory and to accomplish [God's] will."[6]

Easily misunderstood? Yes indeed!

> You will find some Sisters who will interpret naturalness as license—freedom to laugh, to talk, and to act as unrestrained as people in the world. This is not our spirit. We can and must combine our joyousness with the dignity, sweetness, refinement of speech, posture, and grace that is required of the most austere religious. I am very sure

that the Maryknoll Spirit is one of the most elusive and difficult to cultivate.[7]

Mother Mary Joseph did not use the word *cultivate* for naught. She once cited an example of a Sister who "didn't get it": "I have in mind a Sister with very fine traits of generosity, loyalty and devotion, but a particularly noisy and boisterous person—always wanting to be in the limelight."[8] Mother Mary Joseph reports that when she spoke to her about these things, the Sister naively replied, "I don't want to change. I want to be perfectly natural. This is what I think constitutes the Maryknoll Spirit. It is natural for me to be noisy and I wouldn't know what to do with myself if I were not like this." Mother Mary Joseph's concluding remark: "You see how easy it is for even a [Maryknoll] Sister to get the wrong impression of our spirit?" She urged the Sisters not to confuse things because in the preservation of naturalness "we need to keep all that is fine . . . refine what is rough, and cast out things which are not proper for us as religious."[9]

There was an instance when individuality appeared to trump obedience in the minds of the Sisters. At one point Father Nelson, the vicar for religious in the Archdiocese of New York, had spoken to the community about self-will, and although Mother Mary Joseph does not elaborate on the content of his message, she said that some Sisters "feared they were going to lose that thing that made them 'themselves.' Instead of losing it, we are converting it into something infinitely more precious—following the will of God as expressed to us through others."[10]

Although Mother Mary Joseph stressed decorum, it was not primarily because of an interest in etiquette but for a much deeper reason. "The Holy Spirit," she insisted, "does not dwell in the midst of confusion. If we are to cultivate the Presence of God in our souls, we must realize loud speech and noisy laughter are utterly incompatible with the indwelling of the Spirit." The Sisters were not to do anything to dispel God's gentle, abiding presence. And she concludes, "This is the paramount reason for developing our souls in peace and our manner in quiet."[11]

Mother Mary Joseph was captivated by the mystery of God's presence and tried by every means possible to instill this same fascination in the Sisters. She recognized this mystery of God's presence as the link to universal sisterhood and brotherhood. If God is present to everyone, how can anyone not be awed by the beauty of each person? For this reason she urged the Sisters to balance their efforts to supernaturalize their naturalness by keeping the word *others* in mind.

Along with her instructions on individuality, Mother Mary Joseph often spoke eloquently of the importance of the common good, and she stressed this in her Christmas message to the Sisters in 1928. She had recently returned from her second visitation in Asia and was apparently suffering from bronchitis. On New Year's Eve she sent this message to the community: "If the little birds that are twittering in the branches of my bronchial tree would only hop off to ports unknown, I would have the joy of talking to you tomorrow instead of sending this little message."[12] Although ill, she did not miss the opportunity to recommend to the Sisters that they practice generosity and cooperation in the coming year:

> We must empty ourselves [as Christ did]. In the heart of a missioner there is no time for self, no place for self, outside of making self more and more acceptable to God. And the less we love self the easier cooperation becomes. We cannot stand alone—we are part of a body—we need one another. Let us hunger to serve one another.[13]

She continued this theme into 1930 and beyond. The Sisters were to ask themselves at every turn:

> How do I affect others? What can I do for others? How can I help others? How can I share the grief of others? Think always of others and you won't have time to think of yourself; thus you will discover one of the missioner's necessary characteristics—generosity.
>
> There can be no Maryknoll Sister worthy of the name, who is not heroically generous, generous to the very last inch of her being, generous in the giving of her time, of her talents, generous in her thoughts, generous in every possible phase of religious life.
>
> The longer you live the more is your generosity going to be called upon. If you are selfish by nature, and you do not try to overcome it, you will be a failure in religious life and an appalling failure as a missioner! There is no place in the mission field for the ungenerous soul.[14]

Mother Mary Joseph enjoined the community members to give special thought to the part they played as individuals in the life of the community "whether as a source of strength or as an erosive."[15] She also wanted the Sisters to understand that in community life members no longer act as individuals and that the whole community would be measured by their actions.[16]

She called on the Sisters to think and act constantly on behalf of the common good and stressed that it was not necessary for the Sisters to be brilliant or to have talents beyond the ordinary. Of course, when Sisters were unusually gifted it was a matter for rejoicing, "*in so far as [their gifts could] be used for the good of others*." And she added something from which she never wavered: "There is one thing we do ask of each of you, and that is holiness of life, love of the community, loyalty to the community and a very high sense of your obligations to our community, because it is a very special and particular part of Christ's family."[17]

No one was excused. No one could allow herself to sit back contentedly, letting others look out for the community, saying that it made no difference what she did because she was only one. "Let each one say the same thing and what would be the result?"[18] Each Sister needed to feel responsible for the whole community as if its spirit and well-being depended entirely upon her.

Twenty years later, in 1950, Mother Mary Joseph spoke again to this theme.

> Here our family is very large and I am sometimes afraid that we forget the importance of ourselves in that mass. We think that nobody will notice just one person being out of step or trying to keep out of the limelight so she won't be disturbed—little things like that. We know there are individuals like that in a community. Perhaps we ourselves are such. And yet a group of such persons very soon act like leaven in bread which spreads and very serious difficulties can follow.[19]

The Sisters were always to remember that

> whatever we find in a community of joy and tenderness of one another and thoughtfulness of one another comes from each one of us. A community spirit represents us as individuals. As individuals, we either add to that spirit or take from it. We do not often realize that [our] little mutterings and sputterings . . . can be picked up . . . and passed on to another.[20]

In 1946 Mother Mary Joseph had already elaborated on the paramount importance of generosity and the type of generosity that was necessary for a missioner:

> It is to be a sustained generosity . . . a daily renewal . . . unseen by others and hence spurred by no human help. As time goes on . . . the task requires greater effort of the will . . . supremely tested by apparent failure, by no evident success. It is an effort to fill up a measure

that lacks dimensions, a seemingly endless task, dealing in intangible and variable values, akin to dipping the ocean with a seashell that roused the risibilities of St Augustine. . . . It is a generosity that brushes aside prejudices of race or language or particular converts or agreeable associates or congenial tasks; . . . [it] may require [that] we override our appointed schedule or general rule or the last stronghold of self, our private convenience in matters that are free.[21]

In the same conference, she emphasized that

by the very nature of the work, the missioner must not seek the consolation of gratitude; the task is one of opening ground and sowing seed; it is others who will enjoy the harvest and taste the bread. . . . The only fruit we may enjoy is hope, the fruit of generosity. Our generosity must be blind, unquestioning, confident. It is TOTAL! . . . like Mary's "Fiat." [Jesus' self-emptying, Phil 2:5–11] is the measure of our task.[22]

Mother Mary Joseph was as practical as she was sublime in the matter of generosity and/or cooperation. In 1930, when speaking of the Sisters' daily work, she said, "In the tasks assigned to us we have our hands pretty full and we don't have much chance to do more than our appointed work." However, she insisted there were many little ways in which the Sisters could help one another everyday. It perturbed her to no end that "some . . . go on their own sweet way, looking only for their own end; as a result, they get their work done sooner, which makes the rest of us look as though we were lazy and slow. Surely this is annoying."[23]

And then, with what sounds like a fair amount of frustration, she urges the Sisters to use their heads and keep a balance. "No one is expected to be so cooperative as to be thrown back in her own work. We simply desire that so far as it is compatible with the accomplishment of the tasks given you, that you should sacrifice yourself as much as possible while working with one another."[24]

The Sisters who outdid themselves in their literal interpretation of her every word were obviously a source of great exasperation for her.

In the same conference Mother Mary Joseph told the Sisters that cooperation was particularly necessary "with people placed over you at work. They want it done one way. You want to do it another way. Do it their way! Give in graciously and do not keep insisting that your way is equally as good or better. Make it a rule, that in all things not of vital importance, you yield. It takes strength to yield."[25]

She was careful to add that, when it entailed a matter of justice, if a Sister yielded "just for the sake of avoiding a scene, she was wrong. But, in other matters, always be the one to yield. How much happiness it will give you! It is like oil in a machine. Things run much more smoothly if you keep yourself pliant."[26]

Mother Mary Joseph expressed impatience with Sisters who were prone to offering criticism of others, especially if they themselves did not set a good example. In that case, she said, their criticism was destructive, and she urged the Sisters to address this situation, "sometimes jokingly, though always kindly, get a point across without waiting for the Superior to speak formally. The trouble with most of us," she continues,

> is that we are too self-conscious to bother with others; we are fearful of being considered overly pious when using our influence for good; fearful, too, to initiate improvement, lest we be humiliated. This attitude is not right, nor is it good for us, nor worthy of us, and we cannot hope to attain anything worthwhile so long as this apathetic state marks us.[27]

This discussion ends on a tantalizing note. It may be possible to speculate that as early as 1931 Mother Mary Joseph's holiness, combined with her down-to-earth common sense, was the initial inspiration for the community's future direction in participative governance. "Don't wait for the Superior to speak formally," she had told them. The good of the community was every Sister's responsibility.

In sum, outwardly Maryknoll Sisters were as regimented as any other religious community. Despite appearances, however, each Sister was to cultivate her individuality and thereby preserve her naturalness, so that people would be drawn through her to Christ. In this context Mother Mary Joseph comes full circle in her thinking. To be conduits of grace the Sisters needed to be very conscious of God's presence in them and to realize that the same divine presence is in everyone. This unfathomable mystery linked individuality with common good for her. If God is present in everyone, how can we not be awed by the beauty of each person? And if awed, how can we not be heroically generous vis-à-vis every person we meet? Mother Mary Joseph would have had the Sisters understand that the common good required generosity that was self-initiated (not because they were told), renewed daily (not a once and for all), and sustained (in graced discipline) whether their generosity was appreciated or not, both in community and in mission.

18

The Maryknoll Spirit
of Obedience

When active religious orders were founded in the 1500s, the church mandated that the daily life of active religious should be governed by individuals appointed to positions of trust for the common good, just as they were in monastic orders. These individuals were called superiors. Their authority was delegated by their superior general, and obedience to them was expected of every member. This style of governance remained unchanged until the renewal initiated by Vatican II. Today, many religious congregations have adopted a more horizontal style of governance to foster right relationships throughout the community and to provide a mature environment in which to exercise the vow of obedience, promoting personal responsibility and accountability to the community. This is precisely the understanding of obedience that Mother Mary Joseph envisioned for the Maryknoll Sisters.

During her life Mother Mary Joseph gave more talks to the Sisters on obedience than on any other topic. She desired that the Sisters have a correct understanding of this vow because, as she told the delegates to the General Chapter in 1931, "obedience takes heroic virtue. . . . A community of spiritual weaklings is of no use to God or man."[1]

Although Mother Mary Joseph's lived experience of obedience in community was a pre-Vatican II understanding, her grasp of the deep meaning of the vow was liberating. The importance of the root meaning of obedience[2]—deep listening—was at the heart of her talks to the Sisters. In July 1926 she confirmed the words from Hebrews 10:7, "Behold, I come to do your will," as the keynote of religious life. For her, listening to and doing God's will rather than one's own constituted the essence of an obedience that is true for all people, regardless of their state in life. Each person is called to live in conformity with God's will, that is, with God's help, choosing to do the most loving thing in any given instance.[3] In practice, it means forgetting oneself in the service of others or, in other words, doing the right thing for the common good. While she was on visitation later that same year, Mother Mary Joseph wrote the novices who were soon to profess their first vows: "Learn to love obedience. . . . Obedience is hard because, naturally, we love ourselves and our own wills."[4]

Five years before she died, Mother Mary Joseph returned to the keynote phrase in Hebrews 10:7 and called it

> our theme song . . . the matter of which is as familiar to you as the questions and answers in your first catechism book. We have heard them and all things pertaining to obedience over and over again. We have had them in conferences, we have read about them in our spiritual reading books, and I myself have given you what little I understand of the vow over and over again through the years.[5]

She candidly disclosed that, for her, as for everyone, obedience and the other vows as well were learned over time and through practice. Indeed, there was no other way to arrive at a more mature understanding of the vows. For many years Mother Mary Joseph advocated a practice of obedience that was "prompt and entire and generous—not performed to show the folly of a command, not because we feel incapable, nor because we haven't any initiative. We should always act from a higher motive."[6]

Even when she was no longer mother general, Mother Mary Joseph continued to exhort the Sisters to greater integrity in matters of obedience, but her expectations were not always met. In a conference in 1950 she seemed exasperated: "I don't know who can do anything about [your practice of obedience] except the Lord Himself." She mused, "How wonderful it is to find a house where there is perfect obedience," then paused as she realized, "I don't think I have ever found one, but it is what I feel about it." She described what such a house would be like:

> There you would find, most certainly, a unity because everybody would be acting with one thought and one mind to do the will of God as expressed to them. Then there would be the lovely example of cooperation, humility and understanding of one another, love of one another. There would be an increase of strength in the whole house. There would be a sense of support of one another. . . . We would like our Sisters to feel that herein is their strength.[7]

In a conference given to the community in 1930, she reflected:

I know some Sisters find it hard to keep a good common sense view of obedience. . . . It doesn't make us weaklings; it doesn't take from us the right to make judgments, for we are all bound to form opinions . . . to make plans . . . in regard to our work . . . to give our judgments on certain things, and we are glad to have you express yourself, but the point is this: once the decision is made, forget your own fine plans and judgments. . . . You may be sure that this is a pretty safe guide.[8]

For the greater good of the community, Sisters were expected to comply with a decision even if they did not like it; they were, however, given ample opportunity to add their thinking to the decision-making process. Nowhere does Mother Mary Joseph advocate blind obedience.[9] She made it clear that, ultimately, the decision whether to obey or not was made by the Sister herself but that in most cases, if she did not obey, she forfeited her peace. Mother Mary Joseph also remarked: "I think every discontented person you find in the community is a disobedient person, her whole interior is revolting against this, that, or the other thing, and of course she finds no peace."[10]

Conversely, she was just as careful to counsel the Sisters who were named as superiors:

Although Superiors have the "grace of office," sometimes things elude them. . . . A good Superior is open to suggestions. . . . She ought to listen to them with interest and an open mind. Any Superior who does this and treats her Sisters as mental equals, and reaches out to them with loving sympathy will always be happy, and she will make her household a happy one. . . . Now such a Superior has a right to expect much from her Sisters. . . . We look for Sisters who are simple and frank, docile and obedient.[11]

The first inkling that obedience was emerging as a challenge in the young congregation came in 1926. In a conference to Sisters who were preparing for final profession she said that accepting God's will through their superiors was "a thing our Sisters here find so hard to understand."[12]

That same year Mother Mary Joseph wrote to those who were soon to make their first profession.

The stupendous idea in back of the Vow of Obedience is that we see God in all, not one here or there of our superiors but in all who hold delegated authority. If we can, and we truly must, grasp the idea, and never, never lose sight of it, we shall find obedience supernaturally easy, for, in obeying superiors, we shall be serving God, whom we have chosen as our portion forever.[13]

Mother Mary Joseph noted that from the earliest days Sisters did not hesitate to obey her but questioned the superiors she appointed. Fourteen times, from the years 1926 through 1951, she admonished the Sisters concerning obedience to their superiors. She spoke of "that infernal spirit of independence"[14] that reared its head when some Sisters did not carry out orders or became piqued if placed under someone their own age or younger.[15] However, she also noted that, regardless of age, it was "not at all uncommon for Sisters to rebel against the authority of other Sisters placed over them."[16] She wondered, "Why this [weakness in obedience] is so I do not know. We are all well trained; all know what is the subject matter of our vows and what is expected of us even more through the virtue of our vows. We do not expect vows to be broken. We fail in the perfection of keeping our vows when we do not live up to the spirit of the vow."[17]

Mother Mary Joseph was well aware of natural antipathies in the matter of obeying local superiors. Nevertheless, in 1931 she held that "making due allowance for all natural feelings, we must and do insist that you give obedience to local superiors, as holders of authority, through us, from God."[18] She was relentless on this point, which she had stressed since 1928, because, "Religious life is no place for a woman who will not strive with every power of her soul to erect upon the merely natural, a supernatural structure of virtue."[19] At the same chapter she reflected:

And still we have consecrated Sisters, at odds with a superior, peddling the story of their grievances to anyone who will give ear. This sort of thing spreads like an infection, and a whole household may, through the unwarranted criticism of a disgruntled companion, assume a critical attitude toward a superior. What deplorable weakness and injustice!

With pain in her voice, she continued:

Our line of conduct must be to ignore our merely personal feelings toward a superior, and to see in her the ambassador of God to us. Once, quite of our own accord, we vowed to do this. In failing, we are simply robbing the holocaust, making the already hard road of a superior more difficult, pulling other Sisters down from the plane of their high ideals, all because we have not the moral strength and the good will to make good our pledge, and to hide within our own hearts the dissatisfaction that we feel. Obedience takes heroic virtue. . . . Local superiors are not perfect, at times far from perfect. . . . If conditions under a superior prove impossible, make it known . . . but don't let the community get into the spirit of open rebellion when the difficulty can be handled in a way that is proper and sanctifying.[20]

Nine years later, in 1940, Mother Mary Joseph was distressed because "Sisters will write complaining about . . . things that have happened. . . . While they seldom lose control of their tongues, they pour out venom on paper. The spirit of a person who sits down and writes off things like that is worse than one who loses control of her tongue."[21]

Perhaps aware that she has upbraided the community rather frequently and regularly on the subject of obedience, Mother Mary Joseph tempers her assessment in 1941 with a compassionate word: "When I speak of self-love, lack of obedience . . . those things that injure us all . . . I am mindful at the same time of the beautiful generosity of our Sisters, . . . who give themselves so completely and so generously."[22]

However, after long years of experience, in 1950 Mother Mary Joseph asserted that "Obedience calls for sacrifice . . . for penance, discipline of ourselves."[23]

In understanding the vow of obedience in the twenty-first century the seeds of Mother Mary Joseph's wise counsel hold the Sisters in good stead. She, who always knew that obedience could not be mandated and that the good of the community depended wholly on the good will of each Sister, did not leave them bereft. In her timeless wisdom she counseled:

We do things because we think they are right and not because anybody says we must do them.[24]

Make peace as far as you can. Do not make it because I ask it, but consider the folly of your position.[25]

We pray, not only because it is so ordered at such a time, but because we desire to do so. We work, not simply because we must, but because we love and where there is love there is no labor.[26]

The right attitude toward obedience calls for the same sense of personal responsibility now as it did in the early days of Maryknoll.

Mother Mary Joseph believed in the capacity of the Sisters to mature and to grow in their understanding of the vows. She encouraged, counseled, and reproved them; she did whatever it took to have the Sisters awaken to an obedience that was truly self-motivated. Her common sense and self-discipline are readily applicable to religious life in the twenty-first century. Though Mother Mary Joseph could never have imagined the changes that would come in the wake of Vatican II, through her own gracious style of governance she unwittingly prepared the congregation to comprehend that the meaning of obedience was no different whether mediated through superiors or exercised through horizontal leadership.

As part of the renewal in religious life the Maryknoll Sisters renamed superiors variously as president, councilor, coordinator or co-coordinator, director, facilitator, team member, and so on. Regardless of the title, at all levels of the community these leaders have constitutionally conferred authority as "they endeavor to inspire, encourage, challenge and affirm"[27] the members to live faithfully in their response to mission. The Sisters share the burden of responsibility for the common good as they always have, but now it is through direct participation rather than through superiors. In the spirit of the vow of obedience the Sisters ideally work together to affirm, to question, and to discern with one another in matters of their community life, for the community rises or falls on the willingness and/or capacity of the members to assume this dual responsibility.

Just as in the more traditional understanding of obedience, which required Sisters to accept the decisions of their superiors, obedience still requires heroic virtue, and perhaps even more so in an era where one cannot lay blame on a superior for decisions made. In the absence of superiors, the members of a community must engage difficult personalities and/or seemingly thorny issues. No one is excused. Mother Mary Joseph's statement that "a community of spiritual weaklings is of no use to God or man"[28] has simply intensified. It was for good reason that she urged the Sisters to aim constantly for higher motives, to listen to each other, to participate responsibly in community, and not to cling to their own preferences for the nature of the common good.

When shared leadership was implemented initially in the Maryknoll Sisters' regions in East Africa, a few outsiders glibly dismissed the effort, saying, "It will never work. It requires too much maturity on the part of the members."[29] However, it *has* worked, and the Sisters' experience bears this out. Shared leadership, which calls for a high degree of trust, works only when the Sisters make it work through "speaking the truth in love" (Eph 4:15) or, as Mother Mary Joseph would have it, with "fearless honesty and compassion."[30] In 1952 she said: "The Maryknoll Spirit calls for frankness. You must be frank and open and simple. We don't like anybody who is two-faced. . . . We must be very sincere. . . . This unity of spirit, of heart, and of will which we should cultivate, is really the foundation on which our community life rests."[31] Earlier, she had told the Sisters that "We must cultivate . . . love and trust and patience and tact in our relationships with one another."[32]

A great deal is at stake. Mother Mary Joseph gave testimony to this growth of unity of spirit, of heart, and of will on January 2, 1947, when she left the office of mother general after being the community's uncontested leader for thirty-five years. On that occasion she told the community:

> These have been lovely years in which *we have worked together* and my heart will always sing its hymn of gratitude, to you, for your patience, your faithfulness and your love, and to God, for having given us to each other in this glorious work of the extension of God's Kingdom.[33]

It is clear that, as Mother Mary Joseph formed the community, she responded to the issues that were the signs of her times. She planted the seeds that would nurture the community to the full maturity of

- deep listening to God's will, that is, to what life asks of us at any moment;
- a disciplined obedience that acts from a higher motive, promptly, entirely, and generously;
- honoring delegated authority in the spirit of the vow; and
- common sense and self-motivation in all things.

Regardless of the times and the circumstances, the Sisters are able to call forth the right response only if they have interiorized the virtue through lifelong practice. Mother Mary Joseph often repeated: "Obedience is the most difficult and the most important of our vows. Obedience is the secret of growth of sanctity in any community."[34]

19

Nobility of Soul

The word *nobility* is seldom heard today. It is no longer part of our everyday vocabulary. Yet, the word still carries a certain aura that evokes something that is "above the commonplace,"[1] calling forth the best in individuals. It is a word that embodies the virtues Mother Mary Joseph enumerated in her best-loved and best-known statement about the qualities she desired of a Maryknoll Sister:

> *I would have her distinguished by:*
> *Christ-like charity, limpid simplicity of soul,*
> *heroic generosity, selflessness, unfailing loyalty,*
> *prudent zeal, gracious courtesy, an adaptable disposition,*
> *solid piety and the saving grace of a kindly humor.*[2]

Mother Mary Joseph was particularly fond of the phrase *nobility of soul* and desired that this expansive quality inform the congregational character of the Maryknoll Sisters. Because she thought that nobility, or great-heartedness, was so exquisite a quality she was sure that every Maryknoll Sister would agree that it epitomized an ideal individual.[3]

Mother Mary Joseph gave three conferences that began with the famous quote from James Russell Lowell's poem "Yussouf": "As one lamp lights another nor grows less, so nobleness enkindleth nobleness."[4] She reminded the Sisters again and again that no matter how many other lamps they lit, their own lamp would not diminish. Instead, it would grow into a glorious blaze. The simple act of lighting a candle makes this point obvious; however, it is not always so evident in the matter of self-giving.

Lest her meaning of nobility be misconstrued, Mother Mary Joseph explained that it is not necessary to be highborn or to have achieved high standing in society in order to have nobility. History notes certain personages who, while seemingly favored in many ways, were notably lacking in nobility. As an example, Mother Mary Joseph compared two kings, the sainted Louis IX of France and England's Henry VIII. While Louis's nobility has graced the pages of history since the thirteenth century, Henry's cruelty, lust, and greed in the sixteenth century have consigned him to the perpetual shame of ignobility. She also compares the humble origins of St. Catherine of Siena with the noble lineage of St. Dominic: "Yet both," she says, "are equally dear to us because of their noble qualities."[5]

Experiences in the mission field have exposed missioners to many examples of nobility and the great-heartedness of ordinary people has inspired them to reach beyond themselves. Mother Mary Joseph insisted that Maryknoll Sisters "ought to be in the very highest sense of the word, God's noble women. . . . True nobility . . . is not an accident of birth. . . . We are all children of God by our baptism." She insisted that while baptism made them "heirs of heaven," their vows focused their love on Christ. "Truly," she concluded, they "can claim a noble heritage," but not for themselves alone. "God looks to us to be light to others."[6]

Since the Maryknoll Sisters came into existence not to satisfy their own needs or desires but to be in service to others, it is proper to ask what people have a right to see in them and expect from them. Mother Mary Joseph answers this question by focusing on what she sees as the marks of true nobility: "courage, fearless honesty, transcending charity, gentle courtesy, tender love of God and all God's creatures because of our love of God." It is equally instructive and thought-provoking to consider what people should not see in them: "In the soul of a missioner, of a Maryknoll Sister, there is no place for pettiness, meanness, selfishness, love of power or comfort, no room for uncharitableness or unkindness, or any of those things which mar beauty of soul."[7]

The second mark of true nobility, "fearless honesty," is particularly challenging. What readily came to Mother Mary Joseph's mind regarding this mark of nobility, which manifests itself in the quality of frankness, is perhaps best described by what she says it is not:

Many people pride themselves on what they call their frankness. "Everyone knows just where I stand! If I am upset about a thing, everybody knows it." What are they doing? They are simply unrestrained, just like little children. Just like a beast almost who simply doesn't make any attempt to rein itself in. . . . It is hard to restrain or check a Sister too proud to consult others, and so frank that she takes every opportunity as a privilege to express herself freely on any subject, all of which she considers an honor. Such a person is often cruel and reveals a heart that is proud in its own judgment and intellect, and must act as she wishes.[8]

While daring in her expression, Mother Mary Joseph clearly does not endorse bluntness as a virtue. She proposes that it may be a good thing when people do not have to guess what someone is thinking, but frankness is not license to vent one's feelings indiscriminately. Together with honesty, she admonishes the Sisters to "cultivate . . . love and trust and patience and tact"[9] in their relationships with one another.

One very practical instance when her advice takes on a particular urgency is in personnel matters, especially when it is necessary to make hard decisions. Mother Mary Joseph encouraged the Sisters to face one another with candor and compassion and to have no secret communications that might cause a Sister to feel isolated or alienated. When Sisters approach one another with fearless honesty and compassion, they are speaking the truth in love (Eph 4:15); they are building up the body of Christ.

Many other instances call for fearless honesty, especially in the current style of participative governance in religious congregations, in which all the members share the burden of responsibility for the common good. This is easier said than done. The challenge is not only to tell the truth but to communicate the truth with compassion. Mother Mary Joseph counsels that a Sister can be compassionate toward a suffering Sister only if she really loves her. In January 1952, when she spoke to the novices, she recalled her earlier instruction that fearless honesty needed to be balanced by a transcending charity: "The Maryknoll Spirit calls for frankness. . . . We must be very sincere. . . . This unity of spirit, of heart, and of will which we should cultivate, is really the foundation on which our community life rests."[10]

In a talk to the community in 1938, Mother Mary Joseph stressed that the Sisters needed to be "examples of Christian virtue in a high and eminent degree." And she added what Maryknoll Sisters have found to be true:

> I am very sure that wherever we may be sent, we will be more than once astounded by the greater nobility of soul that we will find in [adherents of other religions] whom we meet—greater than we ourselves possess. That in itself is a condemning fact. They, of course, haven't the light of Faith, the graces that we have, but they have natural, noble qualities, and they are only waiting for the light [of Christ] that we shall bring, to become, themselves, centers of warmth and light and spiritual vigor to others. . . . Unless we . . .

develop in ourselves this loftiness of soul, certainly we cannot in any way be a light to them.[11]

In this same talk she recalled that on Candlemas Day (February 2), the darkened chapel had been ablaze with light after each Sister had passed the light from her candle to the one next to her. "Each light still remains beautiful but has given light to something else and that is the kind of nobility that I desire so much for you. . . . I can wish you nothing better, Sisters, than that you arrive at true nobility of soul fashioned after the likeness of Christ."[12]

In essence, nobility of soul lifts the community above the commonplace. Cultivation of this quality will enable the community to live Mother Mary Joseph's most cherished dream for them as Maryknoll Sisters.

The entire purpose of striving to live up to this ideal is to draw others to Christ. To this end Mother Mary Joseph urged the community to cultivate transparency as described in her first conference on the presence of God. Thus, nobility of soul brings the community full circle, to the taproot of their graced inheritance as Maryknoll Sisters.

20

Ecce Ancilla Domini

(Behold the Handmaid of the Lord)

On the feast of the Annunciation, while awaiting passage back to the United States from the Philippines in March 1930, Mother Mary Joseph wrote to the Sisters at Maryknoll:

This is a great Feast for us, the commemoration of that momentous utterance of our Blessed Lady, "Ecce Ancilla Domini." At the beginning of this new day, a day that holds almost endless opportunities for expressing our love of God, may our hearts be quickened to make generous resolutions to be in truth, God's handmaidens, yielding ourselves unreservedly to God's action in our souls.[1]

Two years later, when the Contemplative Community invited Mother Mary Joseph to assume a cloister name in solidarity with them, she replied spontaneously: "I will be called Mother Mary Joseph of the Annunciation."[2] On the feast of the Annunciation in 1933, in a conference to the community at Maryknoll, she disclosed the awe in which she held Mary's perfect unreserved openness to God: "Is it any wonder that we, who have taken upon ourselves the livery of Christ's messengers, should look upon the Feast of the Annunciation as particularly our own? Our house, our chapel, are dedicated to the Lady of the Annunciation, to this unspeakably great mystery." She continued to reveal the depth of her understanding of this mystery by stating, "Each of us is pledged to bear Christ within herself and . . . show Him forth, as Mary did . . . in this great task which is ours."[3]

For Mother Mary Joseph, it was not only that we should bow in admiration of Mary's *Fiat*. Mother Mary Joseph highlighted the second part of Mary's reply: "Be it done to me according to your Word" as all-important for Maryknoll Sisters. She said that "these words and not the first part of Mary's recital brought God from heaven to earth."[4]

Today, in the twenty-first century, Maryknoll Sisters continue to probe the meaning of their long cherished motto, *Ecce Ancilla Domini*, which was bestowed on the congregation by Mother Mary Joseph. In 1941, she had posed this question:

> What *should* this, our Community, motto mean to us? . . . Words are easily spoken, so easily that we sometimes hardly know the meaning of what we say, and even these breathtaking words, "Behold, the handmaid . . ." "Be it done to me according to your word" . . . even these can return to us void, if they are borne on our lips and not in our hearts.

She gave the community pause when she added: "This morning, as we say, 'Behold the Handmaid of the Lord,' just what are we inviting God to behold?"[5]

To begin to grasp what Mother Mary Joseph held so close to her heart, and how one can enter into the mystery of the Annunciation, it is necessary to turn to the story of Mary's *Fiat* as it is enshrined in Luke 1:26–38. The following close reading of Mother Mary Joseph's understanding and commentary on this passage will be interlaced where appropriate with scriptural interpretation, thus enabling the reader to contemplate the mystery with her.

From the opening verses of Luke's Gospel one is able to sense the evangelist's eagerness to tell the story of God-with-us to his beloved Theophilus. To do so he reaches back into the ancient world of the Hebrew Bible where the Jewish people converse with God as with a neighbor, where it is normal for people to speak in canticles, and where angels, who stand before the throne of God, are also at home among human beings. Luke, artist and theologian, "paints with words on the Christian imagination,"[6] and gently draws us into the mystery of the incarnation.

The gospel scene is peopled with characters of our ancestral faith—human beings who grope for understanding even as they are caught up in God's action and God's time. When Luke finally introduces Mary, the virgin betrothed to Joseph, her place in the foreground is claimed. She stands in front of Elizabeth and Zechariah and behind them, out of the mists of the patriarchal age, are Sarah and Abraham, the first to hear that with God nothing is impossible.

Reflection on the scene of the angel's announcement to Zechariah gives entrée into the depth with which Luke endows the scene of the

Annunciation to Mary. At the beginning of the infancy narrative (Lk 1:5–25) Elizabeth and Zechariah are introduced as husband and wife, both from notable families. They are righteous people, advanced in years and childless (vv. 5–7). With great simplicity and subtlety Luke evokes the story of Abraham and Sarah, another blameless and childless couple who were visited by an angel of the Lord and received the announcement of the forthcoming birth of their son, Isaac, for nothing is too wonderful for the Lord (Gn 18:14).

The following scene focuses on the angel's appearance to Zechariah in the Temple with the news that his prayer has been heard (Lk 1:13).[7] Elizabeth will bear a son who will turn many of the people of Israel to the Lord their God (v. 16). When Zechariah questions how that will come to be, the angel identifies himself as Gabriel, the angel who is associated with the messianic hopes and dreams of Israel (Dn 8:16ff.).

Gabriel appears again when Elizabeth is in her sixth month, only this time in the small town of Nazareth (Lk 1:26). Unlike the Temple, which was the center of Judaism and in continuity with Old Testament institutions, no such traditions were attached to Nazareth. Something new will come from Nazareth.

Not only is the town of Nazareth of no consequence, but the person to whom the angel Gabriel comes is also of no consequence. She is introduced in reference to her betrothed, Joseph of the house of David. After leading us to believe that her status will be derived from her husband, Luke says "and the virgin's name was Mary." A master storyteller, Luke deliberately places Mary's name in the emphatic position so that when he comes to a full stop, all eyes are on her.

The angel comes to Mary, not because of any importance on her part, for as a woman she is among the most powerless in her society. Given this reality, Mother Mary Joseph reflects on God's choice of Mary: "The Creator of the world had not sought a mother in the midst of the grandeurs that dazzle the eyes. The Holy Trinity would find a dwelling for God in the abyss of humility and self-abasement."[8]

Compared with Zechariah, who was righteous before God and who held an official position as a priest, Mary has no official standing; she is not even described as righteous. Nothing is said that would lead one to think she is particularly noteworthy or deserving of honor. Yet, the angel Gabriel comes to her and *twice* in the same sentence she is identified as a *virgin*.

Mary's insignificance is twofold: first, as a woman, and second as a virgin, a "nobody." In Jewish culture, as in many cultures of the world today, a woman only becomes somebody when she becomes a mother. One wonders why Luke puts emphasis on Mary's virginity;

what is its deeper meaning? In ancient cultures, as today, people did not refer to an unmarried woman as a virgin. Luke had many ordinary Greek words at his disposal. He could have referred to her as a girl or a maiden. But his use of the word for *virgin* and its repetition in the text indicates that he did it deliberately. Luke's understanding of *virgin* is not the same as contemporary societies and cultures commonly understand the word. It is vital to probe Luke's meaning in order to get to the heart of the Annunciation.

Mother Mary Joseph marvels that the angel Gabriel comes from God to Mary, "not as the bearer of God's orders, but to ask her consent—to allow her to make a free and willing choice of the most stupendous of privileges."[9] Gabriel's greeting bestows on Mary a new title, "Fully Graced!"

> What praise, and from God's own messenger. We who are so easily flattered, in spite of our sinfulness accept very readily as quite becoming to us, any words of commendation from any person. But not so in the sinless Mary, who was troubled because of heaven's high praise.[10]

No one in the history of the world had ever been greeted this way. Others in the Hebrew scriptures had been blessed—Abraham and Sarah, Isaac and Leah and Rebekah, Jacob and Rachel, indeed, the whole people had been blessed—but no one had ever been called "fully graced" as was Mary.

When Mary heard this greeting, she was perplexed. As Luke unfolds the story, attention is riveted on Mary as the painting is completed one stroke at a time. Throughout the ages many have wondered about the meaning of this message, but what will be asked of her will be possible because, as the angel states, "the Lord is with you" (v. 28). This is the guarantee that God's plan for her will be realized. Mary does not yet know the contours of God's plan, but she knows that she is not to be afraid (v. 30) and that she will bear a son and call him Jesus (v. 31).

One can ask if this is really momentous news since Mary is engaged to be married. Nothing is said about the timing of the birth. Mary could easily conclude that she would conceive after she and Joseph had begun their life together. The message is so ordinary that one may wonder about the extraordinary greeting and the visit of an angel who is associated with the fulfillment of the hopes and dreams of Israel. Luke, the master storyteller, had led his audience to expect something more.

The "something more" is found in God's invitation to Mary to "bear the Son of the Most High." This will be God's work in her as "the power of the Most High will overshadow you." And herein is the meaning of "virginal conception"—it is of God's doing. Through the use of symbolic language, Luke draws the reader into an experience of transcendence—into the mystery to which the virginal conception points: the giving of oneself totally to God, of surrendering before the mystery of God without any reservation. To be virginal means to make oneself available for whatever God will ask. Like Mary, when we, women and men, say yes to life, yes to the giving of ourselves as nourishment for others, we too are overshadowed by the Holy Spirit and our love is rendered generative, like Mary's. The Word of God becomes flesh in us as truly as in Mary, and love is poured out on all whose lives we touch.

Fully cognizant of her utter incapacity to do what God was asking of her and trusting that with God nothing is impossible (v. 37), Mary made herself totally available even when she could not imagine the consequences that her *Fiat* would entail (v. 38).

Mother Mary Joseph expresses the intensity of her entry into this passage:

> And so we follow that breath-taking scene until our listening ears catch Mary's Fiat . . . in her incomparable magnanimity. "Behold the handmaid of the Lord, be it done to me according to your word." . . . The God of infinite patience and unlimited mercy awaits our Fiat, yours and mine and that of all . . . who would taste the sweetness of God's mercy, yet hesitate to pay the price of Mary's words, "Be it done to me according to your word." We are unwilling to give up the little gods we worship, too proud to yield our judgments, too self-loving to sacrifice our wills, too unloving to seek union with a crucified spouse, too cowardly to enlist under the banner of the cross, too soft to tread the road to Calvary. Let us ponder well this thought that God awaits our fiat . . . [to] draw all hearts to Christ.[11]

For Mary, as for all Christians, the initial yes—and every yes—is only the beginning of the road to Christian discipleship.

On the feast of the Annunciation in 1942, Mother Mary Joseph prayed, "Would that Mary gained for us a little of her immense generosity, profound humility, her self-annihilation, her oneness with the Father's will."[12] The following year on Departure Day she gave a meditation on the text of the Annunciation to fortify the commitment of the Sisters who were soon to leave for their mission assignments:

> Let us renew our devotion to Mary in the Mystery of the Annunciation and of the Incarnation. Let us resolve to recall each morning as we come into this chapel, or any Maryknoll Sisters' Chapel anywhere in the world, that it is Mary's house, and that in it we renew, not only our conformity to, but our love of God's Will for us. No matter where we are or what our work is, whether we are ill or well, always we are the "Handmaids of the Lord," ready and eager to do what [God] wills, when [God] wills, and as [God] wills. Thus, and thus only, will we remain a united family, bonded in the love of Christ. . . . May Jesus, Mary, and Joseph help us to fulfill our sacred role as handmaidens of the Lord.[13]

Chronology of the Life of Mother Mary Joseph Rogers

1882	*October 27.* Mary Josephine Rogers is born in Boston, Massachusetts.
	November 13. Baptized in St. Francis de Sales Church in Roxbury, Massachusetts.
1889–1900	Attends Bowditch Public School in Jamaica Plain and West Roxbury High School, Massachusetts.
1900	*June 25.* Graduates from West Roxbury High School; returns in the fall for the fourth year of studies required for college entrance.
1901	*September.* Begins studies at Smith College, Northampton, Massachusetts.
1905	*June.* Graduates from Smith; attends Boston Normal School for teacher education.
1906	*September.* Begins as a demonstrator in the Department of Zoology at Smith; is asked to begin a study class on Catholic missions.
	Mid-October. Writes Father James Anthony Walsh, director of the Society for the Propagation of the Faith in Boston for background materials. On October 4, Walsh and others had launched the Catholic Foreign Mission Bureau to organize literary propaganda to awaken missionary consciousness in U.S. Catholics; first edition of *The Field Afar* magazine is published on January 1, 1907.
	December. Meets Father Walsh at his office on Union Park Street, Boston.
1907	*Summer.* Volunteers her services during the vacation months.
1908	*Spring.* Completes her second year of teaching at Smith and decides not to pursue a master's degree; begins to

	teach at a Boston school and becomes a daily collaborator with Walsh.
1910	*September 15.* Dedicates her life to the work that was about to begin to establish an institute for the formation of missionaries.

In the Meantime

1904	Fathers Walsh and Price meet at Missionary Union Congress, Washington DC.
1910	*September 10.* Father Price seeks out Father Walsh at the International Eucharistic Congress in Montreal; the two decide to start a training institute for missionaries.
1911	*April 27.* U.S. bishops approve "the American Foreign Mission Seminary in the U.S."
	May 30. Walsh and Price seek approval from Rome.
	June 29. Papal approval is given.
	September 19. Walsh and Price arrive back in Boston.
	October. First location for The Catholic Foreign Mission Society of America at Hawthorne, New York.

The Women Volunteers

1911	*June.* Two letters from Mary Louise Wholean await Walsh. She specifies her desire for religious life and for dedicating her life to foreign mission.
	Late September. Sara Sullivan writes to offer her services to the foreign mission enterprise. Other women include Nora Shea, Walsh's secretary; Mary Dwyer, whose business skills Walsh considers invaluable; and Mollie Rogers, Walsh's collaborator since 1907.
1912	*January 6.* Three women arrive at Hawthorne: Mary Louise Wholean, Sara Sullivan, and Mary Dwyer; Nora Shea is still needed in Boston; Mollie is detained at home due to a financial crisis in the family.
	February and July. Mollie visits Hawthorne and meets Mother Alphonsa Lathrop (Rose Hawthorne).
	August 17. Purchase of property for Maryknoll's permanent location on Pinesbridge Road in Ossining, New York, overlooking the Hudson River; gift from Mother Alphonsa frees Mollie to come to Hawthorne.

September 9. Mollie arrives to stay, with Margaret Shea, a new candidate for the "secretaries."

September 15. Two years to the day after Mollie's resolve to dedicate her life to mission, Walsh places her in charge of the secretaries; she begins to be addressed as Mary Joseph.

October 15–16. Secretaries, soon to be called Teresians, move to Ossining to St. Teresa's Lodge on the Maryknoll compound.

1913   *May 1*. Death of Mary Joseph's father.

September 3. Opening of a junior seminary, The Venard Apostolic School, in Scranton, Pennsylvania.

1914   *July 15*. Mary Joseph travels as companion to benefactor Julia Ward, en route to Europe; first stop, Lourdes.

August 20. Arrives in Rome. That day, death of Pius X.

World War I Spreads over Europe

September 15. Arrival at Maryknoll of three Sisters, Servants of the Immaculate Heart of Mary (IHMs) from Scranton; approved by Cardinal Farley of New York and Bishop Hoban of Scranton, they come to direct the novitiate for the Teresians.

October 2. Mary Joseph and Julia Ward arrive in New York.

1916   *March 7*. Father John T. McNicholas, OP, enrolls the Teresians as Dominican Tertiaries, the first step toward religious life; announces that the novitiate year was invalid as per a recent decree that specified that permission to found a new religious congregation had to come from Rome. With this setback Mary Dwyer withdraws from the Maryknoll enterprise. During the years 1913–16, eleven more women join, bringing the total to seventeen, all of whom will remain committed for life.

June. First petition sent to Rome for permission to initiate a religious congregation.

July 1. IHMs return to Scranton; Mary Joseph assumes role of director once again.

August. Petition returned because it had been sent to the wrong office at the Vatican; re-posted.

1917   *January*. Petition to initiate a religious congregation not granted; permission granted only to organize as a society of pious women without vows.

February 19. Mary Louise Wholean dies of cancer.

April 6. Declaration of war between Germany and the United States.

Father McNicholas arranges for Sinsinawa Dominicans to help in the novitiate formation of the Teresians; Sister Ruth Devlin, OP, spends four months at Maryknoll; begins a study program with the Teresians; focuses on tentative constitutions.

August. Walsh undertakes trip to China in search of mission field for first group of priests; before his departure a second petition is sent to Rome.

December 25. Mission field procured in Yeungkong and Loting.

1918   *February*. Refusal of second petition because neither the scope of the work nor the means of support was clearly defined.

July 16. Thirteen Teresians make private vows, and four of them begin their first mission at the Venard in Scranton.

September. First group of Maryknoll priests, including Father Price, leave for China.

November. With the end of World War I, new opportunities open up for the women.

1919   *June 7*. Third petition is carried by hand to Rome.

July 6. In anticipation of a favorable reply, Sister Fidelia Delaney, OP, of Sinsinawa, Wisconsin, comes to serve as director of novices.

September 12. Death of Father Price in Hong Kong from a ruptured appendix.

1920   *February 14*. Official approval received from Rome to become a diocesan congregation, Foreign Mission Sisters of St. Dominic.

April. Teresians begin mission among the Japanese people in Los Angeles and Seattle.

1921   *February 15*. First profession of vows.

	August. Second profession of vows. Professed Sisters now total thirty-eight.
	September 12. First departure ceremony for twenty-three Maryknoll Sisters to Los Angeles, Seattle, the Venard, and the first six to China.
1922	Second group of six Sisters missioned to China.
1923	*February 20*. Death of Mother Mary Joseph's mother.
	September 23. Mother Mary Joseph leaves for first mission visitation to Asia.
1924	*February 11*. With Sister Mary Paul McKenna, Mother Mary Joseph makes final vows in Shingishu, Korea.
	April. Returns to Maryknoll. Sister Fidelia Delaney, OP, goes back to her own community.
1925	*May*. First General Chapter and first election of the mother general and her council for a six-year term; Mollie—Mary Joseph—had been appointed annually by Walsh for eight years, 1912–20; she was appointed as first prioress by Cardinal Hayes until this first General Chapter in 1925; now, elected mother general, 1925–31.
	Fall. Controversy in *America* magazine.
1926	*October*. Second mission visitation to Asia.
1929	*September*. Breaking ground for Sisters' Motherhouse on the property across the road from the Society.
	October. Stock market crashes.
1931	*July 2*. Second General Chapter. Reelection of Mother Mary Joseph. Initiation of a contemplative branch of Maryknoll Sisters.
1932	*March 2*. Sisters move across the road to the newly completed Motherhouse.
	October 3. Formal enclosure of first group of Contemplative Sisters.
1933	*June 29*. James Anthony Walsh ordained bishop.
1935	*Mid-October*. Bishop Walsh's health fails noticeably.
1936	*April 14*. Death of Bishop Walsh; James Edward Walsh succeeds him as second superior general of the Maryknoll Society.
1937	*July 13*. Third General Chapter; reelection of Mother Mary Joseph. In the face of impending war, she plans a

mission visitation to Asia but is denied a passport because of the turbulent political situation.

1940   *February*. Mother Mary Joseph is invited to receive a doctor of humane letters degree at Smith in June; ecclesiastical permission denied.

May 29. Mother Mary Joseph travels with Sister Mary James Rogers, MM, to the West Coast and Honolulu on September 11. From there, despite travel restrictions, they proceed to Asia, where they are only permitted to enter the port cities in Japan, Hong Kong, and the Philippines. On December 29 they begin their return to the United States.

1941–44   *December 7*. Pearl Harbor; a few hours later Japan attacks the Philippines. Expansion of mission to minorities in the United States and to Central and South American countries. During these years Mother Mary Joseph is chronically ill; thirty-eight Sisters are still at work in South China and fifty-three are interned in the Philippines.

1945   *February 24*. Liberation of internees at Los Baños, Philippines.

April 3. Disappearance of Sister Hyacinth Kunkel in the Philippines.

May 29. Mother Mary Joseph is awarded doctor of laws degree at Regis College, Boston.

August. Further expansion of mission among Chinese immigrants in New York and Hispanics in Stockton, California.

1946   *July 13*. Fourth General Chapter (postponed from 1943 because of the war). Mother Mary Joseph reelected unanimously; because the church ordinarily permits two terms only (although there was no question about her third reelection in 1937), a request—called a postulation—is submitted to Rome.

November 30. Postulation denied; Mother Mary Joseph calls an elective chapter.

1947   *January 2*. Elective chapter; Mother Mary Columba Tarpey succeeds Mother Mary Joseph as mother general of the Sisters.

February 11. Mother Mary Joseph goes to Monrovia, California, with Sister Mary James Rogers, MM.

October 7. Mother Mary Joseph is requested by Mother Mary Columba Tarpey to reside at the new novitiate in St. Louis, Missouri.

1948   *Early February*. Mother Mary Joseph returns to the Motherhouse because of illness.

June 4. Mother Mary Joseph gives retreats to the Maryknoll Sisters in Hawaii and returns to Monrovia in the fall.

1949   *November 5*. Mother Mary Joseph is awarded doctor of laws degree at Trinity College, Washington DC. Returns to the Motherhouse.

1950   *June 3*. Mother Mary Joseph is awarded doctor of humane letters degree at Smith College.

1952   *March 23*. Mother Mary Joseph suffers a stroke.

1954   *December 12*. Maryknoll Sisters Congregation becomes a pontifical institute; title is officially changed from Foreign Mission Sisters of St. Dominic to Maryknoll Sisters of St. Dominic.

1955   *October 7*. Mother Mary Joseph's condition becomes critical.

October 9. Death of Mother Mary Joseph Rogers.

Notes

Foreword

1. Suzanne Noffke, OP, "Doing History as 'Sacramental Remembrance,'" Keynote Address to the Dominican Archivists and Historians' Conference, July 8–11, 2010 (River Forest, IL: The McGreal Center for Dominican Historical Studies, Dominican University), 8.

Preface

1. Sister Jeanne Marie Lyons, *Maryknoll's First Lady* (New York: Dodd, Mead, and Company, 1964).

2. Camilla Kennedy, MM, *To the Uttermost Parts of the Earth: The Spirit and Charism of Mary Josephine Rogers* (Maryknoll, NY: Maryknoll Sisters, 1980) (hereafter, Kennedy). Mother Mary Joseph's charism consisted of the gifts manifested in her person and the spirit she passed on to the Sisters in her formation of the community. The Sisters preserve the charism in their embodiment of the Maryknoll spirit.

3. Penny Lernoux, *Hearts on Fire: The Story of the Maryknoll Sisters* (Maryknoll, NY: Orbis Books, 1993).

4. Mary Josephine Rogers, "Tape Commentary on 'Early Days,'" Maryknoll Mission Archives, Maryknoll, NY (hereafter, MMA).

5. Sister Barbara Hendricks was president of the Maryknoll Sisters' Congregation from 1971 to 1978.

6. Barbara's original manuscript of the life of Mother Mary Joseph, together with her essays, is available in the Maryknoll Sisters Library and the Maryknoll Mission Archives.

7. These themes are discussed briefly at the beginning of the essay on contemplation and action.

8. *Ecce Ancilla Domini*—"Behold the Handmaid of the Lord" (Lk 1:38) is the motto of the Maryknoll Sisters.

9. Former Maryknoll Sisters who continue to contribute their time and energy in the service of others.

Part I

1. The Early Years

1. Mary J. Rogers, letter to Father James A. Walsh, October 1906, MMJR [Mother Mary Joseph Rogers] Papers, box 2, fold. 1, Maryknoll Mission Archives, Maryknoll, NY (MMA), Maryknoll, NY.

2. James A. Walsh, reply to Mary J. Rogers, 20 October 1906, MMJR Papers, box 2, fold. 1, MMA.

3. According to a great-grandson, Patrick assumed the name Henry because he thought it would be politically advantageous to be associated with such a famous patriot. See Frank Rogers Callahan, "The Rogers Family Story," unpublished draft, 6 December 1999, MMJR Papers, box 1, fold. 8, MMA. Frank was the grandson of Anna Rogers, daughter of Patrick Henry and Mary Dunn, and first cousin of Mollie. Anna and Mollie were roommates at Smith. Anna graduated a year before Mollie.

4. Much of the information on Mollie's family and its relationships, as well as her experiences at Smith College, was derived from interviews with family members and friends of Mollie. For detailed documentation see Sister Jeanne Marie (Lyons), *Source Book* for *Maryknoll's First Lady*, esp. chap. 1 notes, box 34, MMA (hereafter, *Source Book*).

5. From Frank Rogers Callahan's account, shared with Smith College at the time of Mollie Rogers's centennial celebration at Smith, 27–28 February 2005, MMJR Papers, box 1, fold. 8, MMA.

6. For more background on the personalities of the grandparents and their influence on the grandchildren, see Sister Jeanne Marie (Lyons), *Maryknoll's First Lady* (New York: Dodd, Mead, and Company, 1964), chap. 1 (hereafter, *MFL*).

7. See Callahan, "The Rogers Family Story," 1.

8. Mother Mary Joseph Rogers, "Mission Interest," handwritten article, Seattle (undated, probably composed in the early 1940s), MMJR Papers, box 12, fold. 7, MMA.

9. Rogers, "Blessed Sacrament," 7 August 1930, MMJR Papers, box 10, fold. 3, MMA.

10. For a complete account of this experience, see Part II in this volume.

11. Rev. John Handly, CSP, letter to the editor, *America*, 20 December 1925, MMJR Papers, box 8, fold. 16, MMA. Handly wrote this letter in defense of Mother Mary Joseph Rogers in 1925, at the time when she was strongly criticized by the editor of *America*. In her talk to the Newman Clubs of Teachers' College, Columbia University, and the College of the City of New York, Mother Mary Joseph Rogers had said that her mission vocation could be traced back to Smith College.

12. Rogers, "Foreword," *Maryknoll Distaff: The History of the Maryknoll Sisters*, 1912–61, 4, MMJR Papers, box 12, fold. 8. See also *Source Book*, chap. 2, no. 15.

13. *MFL*, 33.

14. Rogers, "Foreword," 2.

15. See Camilla Kennedy, *To the Uttermost Parts of the Earth* (Maryknoll, NY: Maryknoll Sisters, 1980), 110 (hereafter, Kennedy).

16. Rogers, "Maryknoll Sisters at Home, January 6, 1943" (description of a still film), MMJR Papers, box 12, fold. 5, MMA.

17. "This Study Group finally turned into a Newman Club that persists today at Smith" (Rogers, "Foreword," 6).

18. *MFL*, 44.

19. Ibid.

20. In the 1912 *Teresian Diary*, Mary Louise Wholean's entry of 29 March mentions that she had read the sketch of Theophane Venard's life given her by James A. Walsh eight years before while she was a student at Wellesley. Her interest in foreign mission work never flagged from that moment (box 69, fold. 4, MMA).

21. *MFL*, 60. See also *Source Book*, chap. 3, note 5.

22. *The Field Afar*, April 1920, 90, MMA.

23. On Christmas Eve, 1908, Walsh gave Mollie a bound copy of the first year's issues of *The Field Afar*. On the flyleaf he had inscribed, "To my co-worker with deep appreciation of her faithful service."

24. *Teresian Diary*, 17 August 1912.

25. Rogers, Talk Given to the Community, 6 January 1929, MMJR Papers, box 10, fold. 2, MMA. In this same talk, Mother Mary Joseph mentions that the family used only a small portion of the money and that she was able to turn the rest into the work of Maryknoll.

26. John I. Lane, *Maryknoll Diary*, 1912–15, MMA. Lane, a longtime friend of James A. Walsh, was the first ordained priest to join the Society. See Deceased Fathers' Collection, box 1, MMA.

27. *MFL*, 74–75. See also *Teresian Diary*, 17 and 20 August 1912.

28. Mary J. Rogers, letter to Mother Alphonsa Lathrop, OP, Jamaica Plain, Boston, 28 August 1912, MMJR Papers, box 8, fold. 1, MMA.

29. Ibid.

30. *MFL*, 76–78. See also *Source Book*, chap. 3, no. 69; and *Teresian Diary*, 9 September 1912.

31. Ibid., 80. For further details on the group of secretaries at this time, see *Source Book*, chap. 3, nos. 71–75. Margaret (Sister Gemma) Shea's memoirs written for Sister Jeanne Marie Lyons, 21 December 1955, state: "Father Walsh was not at home when Mother [Mollie] and I arrived but he returned in a few days and gave us a very cordial welcome. It must have relieved him of a big anxiety concerning the 'Group' to have Mother [Mollie] there to take over. Everyone instinctively regarded her as the head of the house" (no. 73, MMJR Papers, box 34, MMA).

32. *Teresian Diary*, 15 September 1912.

33. Ibid. This was the first time Father Walsh referred to Mollie as Mary Joseph. The same *Diary* entry notes that on that same date (15 September 1912) the Teresians celebrated the second anniversary of Mollie Rogers's "formal resolve to dedicate her life to this mission work."

34. Ibid., 16 September 1912, box 1, fold. 1, MMA.

35. According to the records, there were seven women, not eight: Mary Louise Wholean, Sara Sullivan, Mary Dwyer, Nora Shea, Mollie Rogers, Margaret Shea, and Anna Towle.

36. Walsh, excerpt from "Report to His Eminence, Cardinal Gotti, Prefect of Propaganda Fide, Rome, Italy," 8 December 1912, James A. Walsh Collection, box 6, fold. 3, MMA.

2. From "Secretaries" to Women Religious

1. Tradition had it that Teresa saved as many souls through her prayer as Francis Xavier did through his missionary labor. Initially, Walsh seemed to imagine that the women's work might not extend beyond the borders of the United States. See *Teresian Diary*, 1913, 79, box 69, fold. 5, Maryknoll Mission Archives, Maryknoll, NY (hereafter, MMA). The title of Teresians, first bestowed by a friend, Father John McCabe, OP, in a postcard greeting, was immediately adopted.

2. Walsh, *The Field Afar* (March 1920), 51, MMA.

3. Ibid., 90.

4. Mary Louise Wholean, *Teresian Diary*, 1 January 1912, box 69, fold. 4, MMA.

5. Ibid., 5 June 1912.

6. Ibid.

7. Ibid., 23 June 1912.

8. Mother Mary Joseph Rogers, "Canonical Foundation," 14 February 1944, MMJR [Mother Mary Joseph Rogers] Papers, box 2, fold. 3, MMA. Mother Mary Joseph Rogers notes that "fears and objections [had been] voiced by many confessors and spiritual directors that the Maryknoll sisterhood was not a permanent organization and therefore should not be chosen as a field of labor."

9. Camilla Kennedy, MM, *To the Uttermost Parts of the Earth: The Spirit and Charism of Mary Josephine Rogers* (Maryknoll, NY: Maryknoll Sisters, 1980), 26–27 (hereafter, Kennedy).

10. *Teresian Diary*, 5 June 1912, box 69, fold. 4, MMA.

11. Julia Ward had been a very successful businesswoman as a couturière for the theatrical set on Broadway. See Sister Jeanne Marie (Lyons), *Maryknoll's First Lady* (New York: Dodd, Mead, and Company, 1964), 96ff. (hereafter, *MFL*).

12. Ibid., 98.

13. Rogers, "Maryknoll History," 21 January 1948, MMJR Papers, box 2, fold. 5, MMA.

14. *MFL*, 103. The practice of perpetual adoration continued for many years.

15. *Teresian Diary*, 17 September 1914, box 69, fold. 6, MMA.

16. Ibid.

17. In addition to the Dominican ideal of contemplation in action, Mary Joseph also recognized the stability of the Dominican Order within the church as well as the flexibility of the rule with regard to mission work. See Kennedy, 88.

18. *MFL*, 108. See also Sister Jeanne Marie (Lyons), *Source Book* for *Maryknoll's First Lady*, chap. 4, nos. 182-85, box 34, MMA (hereafter, *Source Book*); MMJR Papers, box 34, MMA; and *Teresian Diary*, 7 March 1916, box 69, fold. 8, MMA.

19. *Teresian Diary*, 1 July 1916, box 69, fold. 8, MMA.

20. Ibid., 24 May 1916.

21. *MFL*, 109-10. See also *Source Book*, chap. 4, nos. 185, 189.

22. Walsh, Eulogy preached on Mary Louise Wholean, February 1917, Maryknoll Sisters Necrology, MMA.

23. Ibid.

24. *MFL*, 114.

25. *MFL*, 110. See also *Source Book*, chap. 4, no. 197.

26. Rogers, *Personal Notebook, Chronicle, 1912-1925*, entry for 19 July 1918, MMJR Papers, box 7, fold. 4, MMA.

27. Rogers, "Foundation Day," 14 February 1940, MMJR Papers, box 10, fold. 8, MMA.

28. Rogers [Mary Joseph], letter to Father James A. Walsh, 16 March 1918, Maryknoll, NY, MMJR Papers, box 2, fold. 1, MMA.

29. Rogers, *Personal Notebook, Chronicle, 1912-1925*, entries for 5 March, 4 and 7 June 1919, MMJR Papers, box 7, fold. 4, MMA.

30. Ibid., entry for 16 June 1919, MMJR Papers, box 7, fold. 4, MMA.

31. Walsh, "Foundation Day Talk, 29 June 1935," in *Discourses of James Anthony Walsh, 1890-1936* (Maryknoll, NY: Maryknoll Fathers), 489. Price's body remained in Happy Valley Cemetery, Hong Kong, until the death of Walsh in 1936. At that time the remains of the co-founders were interred at Maryknoll, New York. See Robert E. Sheridan, *The Founders of Maryknoll* (Maryknoll, NY: The Catholic Foreign Mission Society of America, 1980), 96.

32. Patrick Joseph Hayes, Archbishop of New York, document regarding "Erecting into a Diocesan Religious Institute, the Pious Society of Women Who Carry on the Work at the Seminary at Maryknoll," dated 14 February 1920, Maryknoll Congregation Foundation Collection, box 1, fold. 9, MMA.

33. The title of the Congregation was subsequently changed to Maryknoll Sisters of St. Dominic in 1954 when the Congregation became a pontifical institute under the Congregation for the Evangelization of Peoples. But see Constitutions of the Maryknoll Sisters, 14 February 1990 edition, x. In Correspondence with the Holy See, box 1, fold. 14, MMA.

34. Louis Theissling, master general of the Order of Friars Preachers, Rome, Italy, document that recognized the canonical foundation of the Foreign Mission Sisters of St. Dominic by Archbishop Hayes of New York and formally aggregated to the Dominican Order of the Sisters at Maryknoll (signed by Father Leonard Lehu, Vic. Mag. Gen. OP), dated 10 June 1920, Maryknoll Congregation Foundation Collection, box 1, fold. 9, MMA.

35. James E. Walsh, letter to James A. Walsh, *The Field Afar* (July 1920), 154, MMA.

36. Rogers, "Foundation Day." Mother Mary Joseph Rogers recapitulated this same idea in the meditation she gave the community on this same date in 1944, box 11, fold. 3, MMA.

3. The Field Afar

1. *The Field Afar*, September 1921, 244–45, Maryknoll Mission Archives, Maryknoll, NY (hereafter, MMA).

2. Thomas A. Breslin, "Introduction," *American Catholic China Missionaries, 1918–1941*, Ph.D. diss., University of Virginia (August 1972), 11–12.

3. Ibid., 12–13.

4. Mother Mary Joseph Rogers, letter to Father James A. Walsh, 10 October 1923, MMJR [Mother Mary Joseph Rogers] Papers, box 2, fold. 2, MMA.

5. Sister Jeanne Marie (Lyons), *Maryknoll's First Lady* (New York: Dodd, Mead, and Company, 1964), 152–54 (hereafter, *MFL*). See also Sister Jeanne Marie (Lyons), *Source Book* for *Maryknoll's First Lady*, chap. 6, nos. 53 and 55, box 34, MMA (hereafter, *Source Book*).

6. Rogers, *China Visitation Diary, 1923–1924*, 12 November 1923 (first section), 26, MMJR Papers, box 12, fold. 9, MMA.

7. *MFL*, 166–69.

8. Rogers, *China Visitation Diary*, 12 December 1923 (second section), 14–19.

9. Ibid., 13 January 1924 (fifth section), 28–30.

10. Ibid., 17 December 1923 (third section), 16–19.

11. Francis X. Ford, "Superior Surprises," *The Field Afar* (July/August 1924), 205, MMA.

12. Ibid., 207.

13. Francis X. Ford, quoted in Jean-Paul Wiest, *Maryknoll in China: A History 1918–1955* (Armonk, NY: M. E. Sharpe, 1988), 101.

14. Jean-Paul Wiest, *International Bulletin of Missionary Research* (July 1988): 134. For Rome's official approval of direct evangelization by the Sisters, see Wiest, *Maryknoll in China*, 103.

4. A Community for Mission

1. Mother Mary Joseph Rogers, "Sister Fidelia," *Maryknoll, the Field Afar* (September 1943), 15, Maryknoll Mission Archives, Maryknoll, NY (hereafter, MMA).

2. Sister Jeanne Marie (Lyons), *Maryknoll's First Lady* (New York: Dodd, Mead, and Company, 1964), 187 (hereafter, *MFL*). See also Sister Jeanne Marie (Lyons), *Source Book* for *Maryknoll's First Lady*, chap. 7, nos. 12–14, box 34, MMA (hereafter, *Source Book*). Listed in the order of their election, the four councilors were Sisters Mary Columba Tarpey, St. John Brown, Mary de Paul Cogan, and Mary Felicita Clarke. Sister Mary Regina Reardon was elected bursar.

3. Paulist Father J. Elliott Ross was Newman chaplain at Teachers' College (Columbia University) and College of the City of New York.

4. *MFL*, 195–97. See also *Source Book*, chap. 7, nos. 50–56.

5. *MFL*, 196.

6. Rogers, letter to the editor, *America*, 19 December 1925, MMJR [Mother Mary Joseph Rogers] Papers, box 8, fold. 16, MMA.

7. Ibid. This box contains a wide variety of letters from religious and laity, some in defense and some in censure of Mother Mary Joseph Rogers.

8. Scholarships were offered by the Religious of the Sacred Heart at Manhattanville College and the Sisters of Charity at Mount St. Vincent, both in New York City, and the Sisters of Providence in Seattle.

9. The property on which the Motherhouse was built had been purchased by the Society at an earlier date. See Camilla Kennedy, MM, *To the Uttermost Parts*

of the Earth: The Spirit and Charism of Mary Josephine Rogers (Maryknoll, NY: Maryknoll Sisters, 1980), 61 (hereafter, Kennedy).

10. *Source Book*, chap. 8, no. 2.

11. Rogers, "Last Day on the Maryknoll Society Compound," 3 March 1932, MMJR Papers, box 10, fold. 6, MMA. It was the day the Sisters moved into their new Motherhouse.

12. Rogers, letter to Sister Fidelia Delaney, OP, Maryknoll, NY, 21 March 1933, MMJR Papers, box 8, fold. 3, MMA.

13. See Part II in this volume.

14. Rogers, "On Manners," July 1931, MMJR Papers, box 10, fold. 4, MMA.

15. Rogers, "Maryknoll Spirit," 4 August 1930, MMJR Papers, box 10, fold. 3, MMA.

16. Rogers, "Talk before Opening of Chapter," 9 July 1931, MMJR Papers, box 13B, fold. 1, MMA.

17. See Particular Rule of the Catholic Foreign Mission Society of America (no date), box 2, fold. 6, MMA.

18. Jean-Paul Wiest, *Maryknoll in China: A History 1918–1955* (Armonk, NY: M. E. Sharpe, 1988), 203–4.

19. *Source Book*, chap. 8, no. 21.

20. In 1997, the "cloistered" Sisters petitioned the General Assembly to be known as the Maryknoll Contemplative Community because their style of enclosure no longer expressed their reality. Although the present community is now very small, it continues to fulfill its purpose as a vibrant source of spiritual energy for all of Maryknoll.

21. Kennedy, 54.

22. Ibid., 62–63.

23. Ibid., 88.

24. Laurence S. Vaughan, MM, ed., "Chronicle of Notable Events in the History of Maryknoll," Maryknoll, NY, 1 November 1990, MMA.

25. There were 157 priests, 265 students, 68 Brothers, 457 Sisters. See *The Field Afar* (July/August 1933), 162–63, MMA.

26. *MFL*, 212–14. See also *Source Book*, chap. 8, nos. 35–36, 38. For further information about the last years of James Anthony Walsh, see Daniel Sargent, *All the Day Long: James Anthony Walsh, Cofounder of Maryknoll* (New York: Longmans, Green and Company, 1941), 234–48 and passim.

27. Patrick J. Ford, note to Mother Mary Joseph Rogers, Brooklyn, NY, 15 September 1952, MMJR Papers, box 8, fold. 13, MMA. Patrick Ford, the father of Bishop Francis X. Ford, who was imprisoned in South China by the Communists and died there in 1952, wrote her that his son had looked to her as a "spiritual mother."

28. Walsh, letter to Mother Mary Joseph, Maryknoll, NY, 27 October 1935, MMJR Papers, box 2, fold. 5, MMA.

29. Walsh, letter to the Maryknoll Sisters, Maryknoll, NY, April 1936. Texts of Walsh's letters to each group of Maryknollers can be found in Sargent, *All the Day Long*, 242–47.

30. Rogers, "Out of the Years," *The Field Afar* (May 1936), 140–43, MMA.

5. Last of the Founders

1. Laurence S. Vaughan, MM, ed., "Chronicle of Notable Events in the History of Maryknoll," 22 May 1927, Maryknoll Mission Archives, Maryknoll, NY (hereafter, MMA).

2. Bishop James E. Walsh, "Address to the General Chapter," Maryknoll Sister delegates, 13 July 1937, MMJR [Mother Mary Joseph Rogers] Papers, box 13B, fold. 9, MMA.

3. Mother Mary Joseph Rogers, "Talk to General Chapter," 13 July 1937, MMJR Papers, box 13B, fold. 6, MMA.

4. Ibid. "Father General [James Anthony Walsh] thought of utilizing us for anything that was needed . . . of our giving . . . the clerical and other help the newly formed Society needed, and also the possibility of our acting as a society which, by making the needs of the work known, would be a sort of channel through which aid of various kinds would come to Maryknoll Fathers' missions."

5. Ibid.

6. Rogers, "On Religious Life," talk to novices and postulants, 31 January 1929, MMJR Papers, box 10, fold. 2, MMA.

7. Jean-Paul Wiest, *Maryknoll in China: A History 1918–1955* (Armonk, NY: M. E. Sharpe, 1988), 103.

8. Sister Jeanne Marie (Lyons), *Maryknoll's First Lady* (New York: Dodd, Mead, and Company, 1964), 229 (hereafter, *MFL*). See also Sister Jeanne Marie (Lyons), *Source Book* for *Maryknoll's First Lady*, chap. 9, no. 14, box 34, MMA (hereafter, *Source Book*).

9. Rogers, letter to Maryknoll Sisters, Maryknoll, NY, Lent 1938, MMJR Papers, box 3, fold. 3, MMA. See also *Source Book*, chap. 9, no. 14, which contains one section of this letter.

10. *MFL*, 232. See also *Source Book*, chap. 9, nos. 36–37.

11. Rogers, *Visitation Diary, 1940–1941* (visitation to Asia, typescript with handwritten annotations), 8, MMJR Papers, box 12, fold. 13, MMA.

12. Ibid., 7–9.

13. Ibid., 30 January 1941.

14. *MFL*, 240–41.

6. World War II, 1941–1945

1. Sister Jeanne Marie (Lyons), *Maryknoll's First Lady* (New York: Dodd, Mead, and Company, 1964), 241 (hereafter, *MFL*).

2. Ibid., 281.

3. Mother Mary Joseph Rogers, "The Magi, Seeing the Star . . . ," 6 January 1945, MMJR [Mother Mary Joseph Rogers] Papers, box 11, fold. 3, Maryknoll Mission Archives, Maryknoll, NY (hereafter, MMA).

4. Ibid.

5. This information is based on an article written by Sister Carmencita Gabriel, MM, for *The Field Afar*, November 1945, 6–8, MMA. See also *MFL*, 261–62.

6. *MFL*, 262–63. See also Sister Jeanne Marie (Lyons), *Source Book* for *Maryknoll's First Lady*, chap. 9, nos. 170–71, box 34, MMA.

7. Rogers, "Christmas Eve," 24 December 1945, MMJR Papers, box 11, fold. 3, MMA.

7. God Has Yet a Great Work for Us to Do

1. Mother Mary Joseph Rogers, Letter of Convocation for fourth General Chapter, 8 February 1946, MMJR [Mother Mary Joseph Rogers] Papers, box 13C, fold. 1, Maryknoll Mission Archives, Maryknoll, NY (hereafter, MMA).

2. Rogers, "Opening Day of General Chapter," 13 July 1946, MMJR Papers, box 13C, fold. 2, MMA.

3. Rogers, letter on "the Eve of a Sixty-fourth Birthday" to the Maryknoll Sisters, 26 October 1946, MMJR Papers, box 3, fold. 10, MMA.

4. Ibid.

5. Rogers, "First Sunday of Advent," 1 December 1946, MMJR Papers, box 11, fold. 4, MMA.

6. Rogers, "Meditation" (Morning of Elective Chapter), 2 January 1947, MMJR Papers, box 11, fold. 4, MMA.

7. Ibid.

8. Rogers, letter to the Maryknoll Sisters, 5 February 1947, written one week before she left the Motherhouse for Monrovia, CA, MMJR Papers, box 3, fold. 11, MMA.

9. Sister Jeanne Marie (Lyons), *Source Book* for *Maryknoll's First Lady*, chap. 10, no. 22, box 34, MMA (hereafter, *Source Book*).

10. Rogers, letter to the Maryknoll Sisters, "My Dearly Beloved," 14 August 1947, MMJR Papers, box 3, fold. 11, MMA.

11. *Source Book*, chap. 10, nos. 1–63. General letters of Mother Mary Joseph to the Sisters at this time of her life reflect the warm quality of her relationships with them (MMJR Papers, box 3, fold. 10 and 11).

12. Sister Jeanne Marie (Lyons), *Maryknoll's First Lady* (New York: Dodd, Mead, and Company, 1964), 278–79 (hereafter, *MFL*).

13. Mother Mary Joseph's talks, retreats, and meditations, given at the Motherhouse, Valley Park, Missouri, and in Hawaii during the last years of her life are listed in *Source Book*, chap. 10, nos. 55–56.

14. *MFL*, 301–2. See also *Source Book*, chap. 10, no. 142. Mother Mary Joseph Rogers had already been honored by Regis College in Boston in 1945, when the degree of Doctor of Laws was conferred on her. A second Doctor of Laws degree from Trinity College, Washington DC, followed in 1949. See also *Source Book*, chap. 10, nos. 143–44.

15. Jean-Paul Wiest, *Maryknoll in China: A History 1918–1955* (Armonk, NY: M. E. Sharpe, 1988), 388–90.

16. *MFL*, 280–81. See also *Source Book*, chap. 10, nos. 75–76.

17. Rogers, "Obedience," 12 December 1950, MMJR Papers, box 3, fold. 11, MMA. When Sister Joan Marie Ryan was released and arrived in Hong Kong in September 1952, it was from her that Maryknoll heard the news of Bishop Francis X. Ford's death in the Canton prison in February of that year.

18. *MFL*, 306–8.

19. Ibid., 308–9. For some time yet she was still unable to stand or get into a car.

8. As One Lamp Lights Another

1. Mother Mary Joseph Rogers, letter, "My Dear Sisters," 30 July 1954, MMJR [Mother Mary Joseph Rogers] Papers, box 3, fold. 12, Maryknoll Mission Archives, Maryknoll, NY (hereafter, MMA).

2. Mother Mary Columba Tarpey, letter, 20 October 1955, personal file of Mother Mary Columba Tarpey, MMA, 6–7. See also Sister Jeanne Marie (Lyons), *Maryknoll's First Lady* (New York: Dodd, Mead, and Company, 1964), 318–19; and Sister Jeanne Marie (Lyons), *Source Book* for *Maryknoll's First Lady*, chap. 11, no. 57, box 34, MMA.

3. Wherever this quote appears in MMJR's writings, invariably the last phrase reads: and the saving grace of a *sense* of humor. Once, however, on a small card written in MMJR's own hand, on 24 June 1935, it reads: and the saving grace of a *kindly* humor.

4. Rogers, 1 June 1938, MMJR Papers, box 10, fold. 7, MMA.

5. From the poem "Yussouf" by James Russell Lowell.

9. Epilogue

1. See Margaret R. Brennan, IHM, *What Was There for Me Once* (Montreal: Novalis Publishing, 2009), 50; and Kenneth Briggs, *Double Crossed: Uncovering the Catholic Church's Betrayal of American Nuns* (New York: Doubleday, 2006), 50.

2. See Briggs, *Double Crossed*, 47. For a good overview of this movement, see chap. 3.

3. Cardinal Suenens, *The Nun in the World* (London: Burns and Oates, 1962).

4. Brennan, *What Was There for Me Once*, 183.

5. "Experimentation"—the shadowland in which Sisters lived between one form of being and living until the new emerged.

Part II

10. The American Foreign Mission Context at the Turn of the Twentieth Century

1. Gerald H. Anderson, "American Protestants in Pursuit of Missions: 1886–1986," *International Bulletin of Missionary Research* 12, no. 3 (1988): 98.

2. *Dictionary of Christianity in America*, s.v. "Missions, Evangelical Foreign," and "Missions, Protestant Mainline Foreign," ed. Daniel G. Reid (Downers Grove, IL: InterVarsity Press, 1990).

3. Dana L. Robert, "Introduction," *American Women in Mission: A Social History of Their Thought and Practice* (Macon, GA: Mercer University Press, 1996), xvii–xviii. Robert goes on to explain that in the United States the women's

missionary movement peaked in 1910 with the fiftieth jubilee celebration of separate women's mission boards. After that, the trend to merge with male-dominated denominational structures reasserted itself.

4. Anderson, "American Protestants in Pursuit of Missions," 98. See also R. Pierce Beaver, "Missionary Motivation through Three Centuries," in *Reinterpretation in American Church History*, ed. Jerald C. Brauer (Chicago: University of Chicago Press, 1968), 141ff.

5. Dana L. Robert, "The Legacy of Arthur Tappan Pierson 1837–1911," *International Bulletin of Missionary Research* 8, no. 3 (1984): 120–22. I am indebted to Robert for the material in this and the following paragraph.

6. Anderson, "American Protestants in Pursuit of Missions," 101, where he quotes John R. Mott, "History of the Student Volunteer Movement for Foreign Missions (Chicago: SVMFM, 1892), 6–11. See also Dana L. Robert, "The Origin of the Student Volunteer Watchword: 'The Evangelization of the World in This Generation,'" *International Bulletin of Missionary Research* 10, no. 4 (1986): 146ff.

7. Clara Winifred Newcomb, "Concerning Foreign Missionaries," *The Smith Alumnae Quarterly* 2, no. 2 (January 1911), 89–91. The article ends with a complete list of all of Smith's missionary women, including their countries and dates of mission, from 1882 through 1911. Clara Newcomb (1906) and Mollie Rogers (1905) were contemporaries at Smith.

8. Ibid. Newcomb mentions Mary B. Daniels (1882), who died in Japan after twenty-seven years as a teacher and evangelist; and Clara Converse (1883), who was still principal of a school in Japan in 1911 when Newcomb's article was written.

9. It is not known how this came about—whether students volunteered to offer classes—but it is reasonable to suppose that the example of Mollie's Protestant classmates prompted her to present a class on the Catholic experience.

10. "Smith College Mission Study Classes, 1903–1904," flier, Smith College Archives, Northampton, Massachusetts.

11. Ibid.

12. Mother Mary Joseph Rogers, "The Student Volunteers," a talk to the League of the Sacred Heart in Seattle, November 1917, MMJR [Mother Mary Joseph Rogers] Papers, box 12, fold. 1, MMA.

13. "All drop down together" referred to the death of any family member, wishing that no one should go without the others.

14. Rogers, "The Student Volunteers."

15. Rogers, "Foreword," *Distaff: The History of the Maryknoll Sisters*, 1953, MMJR Papers, box 12, fold. 8, 3, MMA. Shortly after writing this foreword, Mother Mary Joseph suffered a stroke and was unable to continue. The project was completed by Sisters Eunice Tolan, MM, and Mary Incarnata Farrelly, MM, in 1970.

16. Sister Jeanne Marie (Lyons), *Maryknoll's First Lady* (New York: Dodd, Mead, and Company, 1964), 196. The only extant reference to Mother Mary

Joseph's talk is the news release in *The Catholic Sun*, December 31, 1925. She is quoted as having said: "It is my honest conviction that if I did not go to Smith College, I should not now be Mother Joseph." For this statement, she was severely censured by the editor of *America* (December 19, 1925). See pages 28–29 in this volume for details of this controversy.

17. Rogers, "Notes from Chapter Talk Given by Mother," 6 May 1940, MMJR Papers, box 13A, fold. 3, MMA. Mother Mary Joseph had just shared with the community that Archbishop Spellman, after conferring with Bishop O'Leary of Springfield, Massachusetts, had denied her permission to accept an honorary degree from Smith College.

11. The Catholic Awakening

1. For background on the Catholic Church in the United States, see Thomas Bokenkotter, *A Concise History of the Catholic Church*, rev. exp. ed. (New York: Doubleday, 2004), esp. chap. 31.

2. Angelyn Dries, "The Foreign Mission Impulse of the American Catholic Church, 1893–1925," in *International Bulletin of Missionary Research* 15, no. 2 (April 1991): 61–62.

3. Ibid., 62.

4. Following the annual meeting of archbishops in October 1897 in Washington DC, the Society for the Propagation of the Faith was organized in the Archdiocese of Boston with Rev. Joseph V. Tracy as its first director. James A. Walsh succeeded him in 1903. See JAW [James A. Walsh] Discourses, box 3, fold. 12, pp. 1 and 8, Maryknoll Mission Archives, Maryknoll, NY (hereafter, MMA).

5. Laurence S. Vaughan, MM, *Chronicle of Notable Events in the History of Maryknoll According to Year* (Maryknoll, NY: Maryknoll News, April 1904), 3, MMA.

6. In 1910, just before the two priests came together to establish the Catholic Foreign Mission Society of America, Price wrote Walsh from Nazareth, North Carolina, 16 October 1910: "Almost as far back as I can remember, I have had two attractions in my life—one to do what I could for the conversion of North Carolina, the other was the foreign mission work with the possibility of dying a martyr in it. . . . Once the work were on an assured basis I would wish to go on in the foreign missions myself when I trust that God would grant my daily prayer for martyrdom." See TFP [Thomas Frederick Price] Papers, box 12, fold. 4, MMA.

7. Vaughan, *Chronicle of Notable Events in the History of Maryknoll*, 3. The three priests were J. F. Stanton; Joseph Bruneau, SS; and J. I. Lane. Lane (b. December 16, 1863) joined the Maryknoll enterprise in Hawthorne, and just before his death on April 24, 1919, Father Walsh received him into the Society. See Deceased Fathers' Collection, box 1, MMA.

8. Ibid.

9. Ibid., 4.

10. This congregation was renamed Congregation for the Evangelization of Peoples by Pope John Paul II in 1982, probably because of the negative conno-

tation the word *propaganda* acquired from the nationalistic propaganda campaigns of World War I.

11. Walsh, "American Catholics and Foreign Mission," address delivered at the Eighth National Convention, Catholic Students' Mission Crusade, Cincinnati, Ohio, printed in New York, 28 September 1933, 4, MMA.

12. In a speech in 1903, the newly appointed James Anthony Walsh outlined the purpose of the Society for the Propagation of the Faith (JAW Discourses, box 3, fold. 12, p. 11, MMA).

13. Americanism was a label applied by conservative Catholics to progressive Catholics in the United States. Leo XIII referred to this label in his letter to Cardinal Gibbons, *Testem Benevolentiae*, in early February 1899, in which he decried the tendency of the church in the United States to adopt progressive American approaches in evangelization. See Bokenkotter, *A Concise History of the Catholic Church*, 376–77.

14. Dries, "The Foreign Mission Impulse of the American Catholic Church, 1893–1925," 64.

15. The Catholic Students Mission Crusade was founded in Techny, Illinois, in February 1918. See Dana L. Robert, *American Women in Mission: A Social History of Their Thought and Practice* (Macon, GA: Mercer University Press, 1996), 347–48.

16. Walsh, "American Catholics and Foreign Mission," 3, MMA.

17. Ibid.

18. Dries, "The Foreign Mission Impulse of the American Catholic Church, 1893–1925," 63.

19. Ibid.

12. Mollie's Path to Maryknoll

1. Deering Hanscom was faculty adviser of the Smith College Association for Christian Work. See Sister Jeanne Marie (Lyons), *Maryknoll's First Lady* (New York: Dodd, Mead, and Company, 1964), 33 (hereafter, *MFL*).

2. Mary J. Rogers [Mollie], letter to Father James A. Walsh, Smith College, Northampton, MA, October 1906, MMJR [Mother Mary Joseph Rogers] Papers, box 2, fold. 1, Maryknoll Mission Archives, Maryknoll, NY (hereafter, MMA). Emphasis added.

3. Walsh, letter to Mary J. Rogers [Mollie], Society for the Propagation of the Faith, Boston, MA, 20 October 1906, MMJR Papers, box 2, fold. 1, MMA. Emphasis added.

4. Rogers, "The Student Volunteers," MMJR Papers, box 12, fold. 1, MMA.

5. Rogers, "Foreword," *Maryknoll Distaff: The History of the Maryknoll Sisters*, MMJR Papers, box 12, fold. 8, 6, MMA.

6. Ibid., 7.

7. *Teresian Diaries*, 15 September 1912, 67, box 1, fold. 1, MMA. Mollie had just been named head of the household in Hawthorne. "It happens by a strange coincidence that it is just two years ago today that Mollie made a formal resolve to devote herself to this work."

13. Mother Mary Joseph Rogers's Mission Vision

1. *Teresian Diaries*, 5 June 1912, box 1 , fold. 1, Maryknoll Mission Archives, Maryknoll, NY (hereafter, MMA). Over time, the entire group came to the realization that to continue, they would have to organize into a stable entity. For the group's development, see Part I in this volume; see also James A. Walsh, "Report to His Eminence, Cardinal Gotti, Prefect of Propaganda Fide, Rome, Italy," 8 December 1912, James A. Walsh Collection, box 6, fold. 3, MMA.

2. Dana L. Robert, "Introduction," *American Women in Mission: A Social History of Their Thought and Practice* (Macon, GA: Mercer University Press, 1996), 375. "As auxiliaries, women religious were expected to be the support staff for the priest-evangelist. . . . Charitable and educational work were essential to the Catholic presence, but were considered auxiliary or secondary to the work of the priest." Throughout her conferences Mother Mary Joseph herself continued to refer to the Sisters as auxiliaries.

3. In the pages of *The Field Afar* Walsh had foreseen the women's place in Maryknoll as follows: "to spread, in this country, a love for foreign missions, and in God's good time to supply laborers for the field afar" (July 1914, 13); "to fit them for a useful career as women auxiliaries to the Catholic Foreign Mission Society of America" (October 1914, 10). He stressed that "all their activities are counting directly for . . . the welfare of the Seminary" (September 1915, 141).

4. Her name was bestowed by James Anthony Walsh, who probably thought it more fitting, given her status as leader of the group.

5. Mother Mary Joseph Rogers, letter to Father James A. Walsh, Canton, China, 23 October 1923, MMJR [Mother Mary Joseph Rogers] Papers, box 2, fold. 2, MMA.

6. Rogers, "Mission Policy, August 17, 1929," MMJR Papers, box 12, fold. 1 (a), MMA.

7. The committee, which was chaired by Sister Mary Paul McKenna, included Sisters Mary Columba Tarpey, Mary Veronica Hartman, Mary Genevieve Beez, Mary Regina Reardon, and Mary Clement Quinn (MMJR Papers, box 12, fold. 1, MMA).

8. Rogers, "Talk to Professed Sisters," 30 August 1931, MMJR Papers, box 10, fold. 4, MMA.

9. Kenneth Briggs, *Double Crossed: Uncovering the Catholic Church's Betrayal of American Nuns* (New York: Doubleday, 2006), 44. Briggs states further: "Many of the questions [in the renewal called by Vatican II] were deeply theological—and as such, nuns were generally poorly educated to handle them. . . . [As recently as] a decade before Vatican II, the only place women could study theology was at St. Mary's College in South Bend, IN, where the enterprising Sister Madeleva Wolff had begun granting doctorates in sacred studies to women in the 1940s" (106).

10. Rogers, "Talk before Opening of Chapter," 9 July 1931, MMJR Papers, box 10, fold. 4, MMA.

11. Rogers, "Expectation of Our Lady," 18 December 1944, MMJR Papers, box 11, fold. 3, MMA.

12. Rogers, "Maryknoll Spirit," 4 August 1930, MMJR Papers, box 10, fold. 3, MMA.

13. Letter of Mother Mary Joseph to Francis X. Ford, 1 February 1935, quoted in Jean-Paul Wiest, *Maryknoll in China: A History 1918–1955* (Armonk, NY: M. E. Sharpe, 1988), 103.

14. Letter of Cardinal Pietro Fumasoni-Biondi to Mother Mary Joseph, 30 March 1939, quoted in Wiest, *Maryknoll in China*, 103–4.

15. Maryknoll Sisters Bishop Francis X. Ford Collection, 29 June 1939, "Foundation Day Report on Kaying Missions," box 2, fold. 9, MMA.

16. Anthony de Mello, SJ, *Seek God Everywhere* (New York: Image/Doubleday, 2010), 121.

17. Rogers, "The Maryknoll Sisters' Spirit," undated conference, MMJR Papers, box 11, fold. 9, 2.

18. Rogers, "On Manners," 1931, MMJR Papers, box 10, fold. 4, MMA.

19. Mary Louise Wholean documents the exotic ring Ningpo had for her in her entry of 21 February 1912: "Fr. Fraser of Ningpo, China visited the office and gave us an interesting talk on some Chinese customs and the works of his mission. . . . He was the first missioner from 'the field afar' to visit us—and the first 'real live' missioner I had ever seen" (*Teresian Diaries,* box 1, fold. 1, MMA).

20. On this trip Mother Mary Joseph was accompanied by Sister Mary Paul McKenna; Agnes Cogan, who was Sister Mary de Paul's sister; and two Charity Sisters.

21. Rogers, *China Visitation Diary, 1923–1924,* undated, probably covers 17 December 1932—13 January 1924, section three, 8. MMJR Papers, box 12, fold. 9, MMA.8. MMJR Papers, box 12, fold. 9, MMA.

22. Ibid.

Part III

14. The Presence of God

1. Mother Mary Joseph Rogers, "Opening Conference," 6 June 1931, MMJR [Mother Mary Joseph Rogers] Papers, box 10, fold. 4, Maryknoll Mission Archives, Maryknoll, NY (hereafter, MMA).

2. Rogers, "Perfection," 6 June 1932, MMJR Papers, box 10, fold. 6, MMA.

3. In a conference on St. Teresa of Avila, 15 October 1949, Mother Mary Joseph spoke of how the first group of women came to know Teresa: "We read her autobiography and learned much from it. We grew to have a truly deep and abiding affection for her" (MMJR Papers, box 11, fold. 6, MMA).

4. Rogers, "Feast of St. Teresa," 15 October 1948, MMJR Papers, box 11, fold. 6, MMA.

5. Ibid.

6. Rogers, "Corpus Christi," 1947, MMJR Papers, box 11, fold. 4, MMA.

7. Ibid.

8. Rogers, "The Presence of God," 25 April 1929, MMJR Papers, box 10, fold. 2, MMA.

9. Rogers, "On Prayer," 6 August 1930, MMJR Papers, box 10, fold. 3, MMA.

10. Rogers, "Holy Eucharist," 30 September 1940, MMJR Papers, box 10, fold. 8, MMA.

11. Rogers, "Silence," 3 August 1930, MMJR Papers, box 10, fold. 3, MMA.

12. Rogers, letter of 1 November 1921 to the Sisters on the West Coast and China, MMJR Papers, box 3, fold. 1, MMA.

13. Rogers, "Presence of God," 23 August 1929, MMJR Papers, box 10, fold. 2, MMA.

14. Considerably later in time, in 1976, Rev. George Aschenbrenner, SJ, expressed this same idea: "If we ever knew how intimately God is involved with us and how intimately and totally God would like us to respond, we couldn't take it; we'd be annihilated. This is an infinitely rich mystery. God does not just want our love in our actions, or in some of our thoughts. God is involved in every single thing that is happening with us." This quotation is a transcription from "The Spiritual Exercises of St. Ignatius Apostolic Spirituality, and Discernment," Jesuit Hall at St. Louis University, 3601 Lindell, St. Louis, Missouri 63108, 1976, tape no. 10, in a set of eleven cassettes, slightly adapted.

15. Intentionally or not, here Mother Mary Joseph Rogers evokes St. Augustine's rapturous, "Late have I loved you, O beauty ever ancient ever new! Late have I loved you! You were within me while I had gone outside to seek you. Unlovely myself, I rushed towards all those lovely things you had made. And always you were with me, and I was not with you." See *Confessions of St. Augustine*, Book X, no. 27.

16. Rogers, "Mary as Our Model," June 1930, MMJR Papers, box 10, fold. 3, MMA.

17. Rogers, "On Prayer."

18. Rogers, "Response to Grace," 14 June 1940, MMJR Papers, box 10, fold. 8, MMA.

19. Rogers, letter of 1 November 1921.

20. Ibid.

21. Rogers, "Particular and General Examination," 21 January 1926, MMJR Papers, box 10, fold. 1, MMA.

22. Ibid. In 1972, the *Review for Religious* published George Aschenbrenner, SJ, "Consciousness Examen," in which he explains the method and its usefulness (vol. 31, no. 1).

23. Rogers, letter of 1 November 1921.

24. Unlike the Examen of Conscience that focuses on sinfulness, the Examen of Consciousness focuses on meeting God in all things, helping the practitioner grow in spiritual sensitivity in everyday life. The March 2003 issue of *Catholic Update* published a popular account of the method by Phyllis Zagano. The Jesuits have developed several different approaches to suit different personalities, such as from the point of view of feelings (Dennis Hamm, SJ), or of relationships (Joseph Tetlow, SJ). There is a wealth of material available on the Internet.

25. Rogers, "On the Cloister," July 1931, MMJR Papers, box 10, fold. 4, MMA.

26. Rogers, Opening Talk to the General Chapter Delegates, 13 July 1946, MMJR Papers, box 13C, fold. 2, MMA.

27. Rogers, "The Presence of God," 25 April 1929.

28. Rogers, Chapter Conference for Superiors, December 1941, MMJR Papers, box 11, fold. 1, MMA.

29. Rogers, "Presence of God," 23 August 1929.

15. Contemplation and Action

1. Sister Barbara Hendricks, Essay Six, "The Maryknoll Spirit," in "The Spiritual Heritage of Mother Mary Joseph Rogers," unpublished document written for Maryknoll Sisters, a collection of seven essays (1995), p. 20, box 147, fold. 1, Maryknoll Mission Archives, Maryknoll, NY (hereafter, MMA).

2. Ibid., 21.

3. A charism is "an invisible structuring of corporate space which manifests itself in the indefinable 'something common' that is visible in the attitudes and behaviors of all the members" (taken from Sandra Schneiders, "Leadership and Spirituality in Postmodern Religious Congregations," a presentation given to Leadership Conference of Women Religious, Rochester, NY, 23 August 1997, 8).

4. Hendricks, Essay Six, 21.

5. Mother Mary Joseph Rogers, "On Personal Responsibility and Leadership," 1931, MMJR [Mother Mary Joseph Rogers] Papers, box 10, fold. 5, MMA.

6. Rogers, "Feast of St. Teresa," 15 October 1943, MMJR Papers, box 11, fold. 2, MMA.

7. Rogers, "Saint Teresa, Our Guide and Companion," 15 October 1949, MMJR box 11, fold. 6, MMA.

8. Rogers, "Feast of St. Teresa," 15 October 1943. In a later conference on St. Teresa, Mother Mary Joseph specifies that in her work of reform, Teresa "traveled about in inclement weather, heat, cold, and rain, over rough roads and often quite unwell and exhausted" (Rogers, "Feast of St. Teresa," 15 October 1948, MMJR Papers, box 11, fold. 6, MMA).

9. Rogers, "Marys of Maryknoll," an article Mother Mary Joseph wrote for *The Field Afar* in 1922. The article is located in MMJR Discourses, vol. 2, 435, MMA. In this article Mother Mary Joseph states that James Anthony Walsh had conferred that title "on the nameless group of secretaries who had volunteered their services."

10. Rogers, "Saint Teresa, Our Guide and Companion."

11. Rogers, "Marys of Maryknoll."

12. Rogers, "Feast of St. Teresa," 15 October 1948.

13. Rogers, "Marys of Maryknoll." See also Rogers, "Maryknoll History," talks to novices in Valley Park, Missouri, 1948, MMJR Papers, box 11, fold. 4, MMA.

14. Rogers, "Feast of St. Teresa," 15 October 1948.

15. Donald Goergen, OP, of St. Dominic Priory, St. Louis, clarified that (wording slightly adapted): "The basis for Dominican spirituality is the contemplation. '*Contemplari*' comes first, then the '*tradere*.' So we are *active contemplatives*. Our

basis and foundation is the contemplative out of which the ministry flows. So, I would prefer 'action in contemplation'" (email, 20 April 2010).

16. Rogers, "The Presence of God," 25 April 1929, MMJR Papers, box 10, fold. 2, MMA.

17. Rogers, "Recollection Day," 3 December 1944, MMJR Papers, box 11, fold. 3, MMA. The Divine Office had been tentatively introduced at the General Chapter of 1931. Mother Mary Joseph reported on the chapter in "Talk to the Professed Sisters," 30 August 1931: "A group will try this out. . . . Our purpose is not to . . . make the daily life any more crowded than it is now. . . . If we find it feasible, we shall work it out in the community" (MMJR Papers, box 10, fold. 5, MMA). After the General Chapter of 1937, there was ongoing experimentation. See "Talk Given by [MMJ] Shortly after the General Chapter in July 1937," MMJR Papers, box 11, fold. 7, and also "Chapter Talk," 1 February 1939 MMJR Papers, box 10, fold. 7, MMA. In a letter on 21 January 1940 she wrote: "I am wondering how the Divine Office is progressing in the various houses— and if its adoption will be practical. . . . I am particularly concerned about the missions where light is so poor and where the Sisters are often on the road" (MMJR Papers, box 3, fold. 4, MMA). By the end of 1944, it had been fully implemented. "To be contemplatives in action and to be closely linked to the Church's life of prayer, we have, for one thing, chosen the Divine Office as a most important help. We have emphasized as far as possible the liturgical customs of the church—our latest effort being sung vespers" ("Recollection Day," 3 December 1944, MMJR Papers, box 11, fold. 3, MMA).

18. Rogers, "Recollection Day."

19. Ibid.

20. Ibid.

21. Rogers, "Talk to General Chapter Delegates at the Cloister," 16 July 1937, MMJR Papers, box 13B, fold. 2, MMA. The Maryknoll Cloister was established in 1932, following the chapter of 1931. Although many people had insisted it would not work to have a contemplative community integral to an active missionary community, Mother Mary Joseph and the chapter delegates went ahead, convinced that it was God's will that there be a few Sisters "set apart through a life of prayer and sacrifice to keep us all on the upward path." In Mother Mary Joseph's vision, the contemplative community was to be a beacon, a constant reminder to all the Sisters of the need to be women of prayer. In this instance she acknowledged that it was a great privilege to meet inside the Cloister, but then added, "It is something quite natural, because it is simply a reunion of the entire family—representatives from all our mission centers . . . with this group of our Sisters . . . who have been set apart. I think one of the great works of the Cloister is to help keep alive [the spirit of prayer and sacrifice] not only in us but in the Maryknoll Fathers as well."

22. Rogers, "Meditation on St. Dominic," 3 August 1934, MMJR Papers, box 10, fold. 7, MMA.

23. Rogers, "Talk to Professed Sisters," 30 August 1931, MMJR Papers, box 10, fold. 5, MMA.

24. Rogers, "First Sunday of Advent," 28 November 1943, MMJR Papers, box 11, fold. 2, MMA.

25. Rogers, "Conference for the New Year," 9 December 1943, MMJR Papers, box 11, fold. 2, MMA.

26. Rogers, "Recollection Day," 3 December 1944, MMJR Papers, box 11, fold. 3, MMA.

27. Rogers, "The Presence of God," 25 April 1929.

16. Unity of Spirit and Diversity of Gifts

1. The author's experience at Hekima College, Nairobi, Kenya, in 1990 is instructive. Before leaving for the General Assembly as a delegate, she told the class of about 130 African women and men novices, plus their formators, who were mainly from Europe, that the Maryknoll Sisters would be focusing on racism in themselves at their General Assembly in October. As she spoke, it seemed to her that everybody had stopped breathing. The air was electric. Clearly racism was a "live" issue—and not only for Maryknoll Sisters!

2. Mother Mary Joseph Rogers, "Community Life," 31 July 1930, MMJR [Mother Mary Joseph Rogers] Papers, box 10, fold. 3, Maryknoll Mission Archives, Maryknoll, NY (hereafter, MMA). Some of the citations have been slightly adapted to fit the context.

3. Ibid.

4. Rogers, "Advent," 5 December 1931, MMJR Papers, box 10, fold. 4, MMA.

5. Rogers, "Fraternal Charity," 29 September 1932, MMJR Papers, box 10, fold. 6, MMA.

6. Ibid.

7. Rogers, letter, "My Dear Sisters," 24 August 1936, MMJR Papers, box 3, fold. 3, MMA.

8. Rogers, letter, "My Dear Sisters," Christmas Message, 1941, MMJR Papers, box 3, fold. 5, MMA.

9. Rogers, "Meditation to Sisters at the Venard," 19 January 1942, MMJR Papers, box 11, fold. 1, MMA. The Venard was a Maryknoll minor seminary in Clarks Summit, Pennsylvania, where Maryknoll Sisters provided domestic services, beginning 18 July 1918.

10. Ibid.

11. Ibid.

12. Ibid.

13. Ibid.

14. Rogers, "Charity," 6 August 1930, MMJR Papers, box 10, fold. 3, MMA.

15. Rogers, "Jealousy," 7 August 1930, MMJR Papers, box 10, fold. 3, MMA.

16. Rogers, "For Superiors," 1931, MMJR Papers, box 10, fold. 5, MMA.

17. "Let her alone," in the sense of not entering into quarrels with her, or being influenced by her negativity.

18. Rogers, "For Superiors."

19. Rogers, "Thoughtfulness," 1931, MMJR Papers, box 10, fold. 5, MMA.

20. This sentence is a reference to Psalm 20:4 in the Douay version of the Bible. See Cruden's *Complete Concordance* (Grand Rapids, MI: Zondervan Publishing House, 1977), where *prevent* means "going before, actually or symbolically." Mother Mary Joseph probably did not elaborate because at that time the Douay version was practically the only one in use and the Sisters were familiar with this translation. "My dear children" was her addition.

21. Rogers, "Fraternal Charity."

22. Rogers, "My Dear Sisters."

23. Rogers, "Fraternal Charity."

24. Rogers, "For Superiors."

25. Rogers, "Talk Shortly after the General Chapter," July 1937, MMJR Papers, box 10, fold. 7, MMA.

26. Rogers, "Fraternal Charity."

27. Ibid.

28. Rogers, "Jealousy," 8 June 1931, MMJR Papers, box 10, fold. 5, MMA.

29. Rogers, "Talk Shortly after the General Chapter."

30. Ibid.

31. Rogers, "My Dear Sisters," 1941.

32. Rogers, "Community Life," 28 January 1952, MMJR Papers, box 11, fold. 8, MMA.

33. Ibid.

34. Rogers, "Meditation," 2 February 1947, MMJR Papers, box 11, fold. 4, MMA.

35. Rogers, "Fraternal Charity."

17. Individuality and Common Good

1. In Mother Mary Joseph's mind the two, individuality and the Maryknoll spirit, were so intimately allied that to speak of one was to speak of the other.

2. Mother Mary Joseph Rogers, "The Maryknoll Spirit," 4 August 1940, MMJR [Mother Mary Joseph Rogers] Papers, box 10, fold. 8, Maryknoll Mission Archives, Maryknoll, NY (hereafter, MMA).

3. Rogers, "On Manners," July 1931, MMJR Papers, box 10, fold. 5, MMA.

4. Rogers, "The Maryknoll Spirit," 4 August 1930, box 10, fold. 3, MMA.

5. Rogers, "On Manners."

6. Rogers, "The Maryknoll Spirit," 1930.

7. Rogers, "On Manners."

8. Rogers, "The Maryknoll Spirit," 1930.

9. Ibid.

10. Rogers, "Obedience," 7 July 1941, MMJR Papers, box 11, fold. 1, MMA.

11. Rogers, "On Manners."

12. Rogers, "The Eve of New Year's Eve," 30 December 1928, MMJR Papers, box 3, fold. 1, MMA.

13. Ibid.

14. Rogers, "The Maryknoll Spirit," 1930.

15. Rogers, "Conference for the New Year," 9 December 1943, MMJR Papers, box 11, fold. 2, MMA.

16. Rogers, "Community Life," 31 July 1930, MMJR Papers, box 10, fold. 3, MMA.

17. Ibid. Emphasis added.

18. Rogers, "Humility," 30 August 1930, MMJR Papers, box 10, fold. 3, MMA.

19. Rogers, "Chapter Talk," 14 November 1950, MMJR Papers, box 11, fold. 7, MMA.

20. Ibid.

21. Rogers, "Opening Day of General Chapter," 13 July 1946, MMJR Papers, box 11, fold. 4, MMA.

22. Ibid.

23. Rogers, "Maryknoll Spirit," 1930, MMJR Papers, box 10, fold. 3, MMA.

24. Ibid.

25. Ibid.

26. Ibid.

27. Rogers, "On Manners."

18. The Maryknoll Spirit of Obedience

1. Mother Mary Joseph Rogers, "On Obedience," July 1931, MMJR [Mother Mary Joseph Rogers] Papers, box 10, fold. 5, Maryknoll Mission Archives, Maryknoll, NY (hereafter, MMA).

2. "In its authentic etymological sense, obedience comes from the Latin, *ob-audire*, which means 'to listen deeply, or from the depths'" (Cynthia Bourgeault, *Centering Prayer and Inner Awakening* [Cambridge, MA: Cowley Publications, 2004], 59).

3. Sandra Schneiders, *New Wineskins: Re-imagining Religious Life Today* (New York: Paulist Press, 1986), 142.

4. Rogers, letter, "My Beloved Daughters in Christ," 5 November 1926, written from Yeng You, Korea, to all the novices, but specifically addressing those who were soon to make their first vows. MMJR Papers, box 3, fold. 1, MMA.

5. Rogers, "Obedience," 12 December 1950, MMJR Papers, box 11, fold. 7, MMA.

6. Mother Mary Joseph Rogers, "Obedience," 4 October 1940, MMJR Papers, box 10, fold. 8, MMA.

7. Rogers, "Obedience," 12 December 1950.

8. Rogers, "Obedience," 2 August 1930, MMJR Papers, box 10, fold. 3, MMA.

9. Schneiders writes that we can expect to find God's will in the ordinary channels of our state of life. But we cannot stop there. We can never abdicate our responsibility. "In other words, 'Blind Obedience' is magic, not faith. It is an attempt to manipulate God by technique . . . the creation and the worship of a strange God" (Schneiders, *New Wineskins*, 148).

10. Rogers, "Obedience," 2 August 1930.

11. Rogers, "Conference to Superiors," October 1940, MMJR Papers, box 10, fold. 8, MMA.

12. Rogers, "Final Profession Group," 26 July 1926, MMJR Papers, box 10, fold. 2, MMA.

13. Rogers, letter, "My Beloved Daughters in Christ," 5 November 1926, cf. note 4, MMJR Papers, box 10, fold. 3, MMA.

14. Rogers, "Responsibility," 5 February 1928, MMJR Papers, box 10, fold. 2, MMA.

15. Rogers, "Obedience," 2 August 1930, MMJR Papers, box 10, fold. 3, MMA. Regarding the subject of seniority there is an instructive paragraph in the 1931 conference, "On Courtesy," to the chapter delegates: "Unfortunately, there has been from the earliest days of Maryknoll, a wrong idea of seniority. We were not responsible for it, nor perhaps were we always conscious of this defect, until, as we began to grow, younger Sisters, better trained and better equipped, were given positions of trust; then the older Sisters found it hard to relinquish places which they considered their due because of longer years of service." Rogers, "On Courtesy," 1931, MMJR Papers, box 10, fold. 5, MMA.

16. Rogers, "Obedience," 8 June 1931, MMJR Papers, box 10, fold. 4, MMA.

17. Rogers, "Obedience," 4 October 1940.

18. Rogers, "On Obedience," General Chapter, 1931, MMJR Papers, box 10, fold. 5, MMA.

19. Ibid.

20. Ibid.

21. Rogers, "Obedience," 4 October 1940.

22. Rogers, "Obedience," 7 July 1941, MMJR Papers, box 11, fold. 1, MMA.

23. Rogers, "Obedience," 12 December 1950.

24. Rogers, "For Superiors," August 1931, MMJR Papers, box 10, fold. 5, MMA.

25. Rogers, "Advent," 5 December 1931, MMJR Papers, box 10, fold. 4, MMA.

26. Rogers, letter, "My Dear Sisters," 26 October 1946, MMJR Papers, box 3, fold. 10, MMA.

27. Constitutions of the Maryknoll Sisters of St. Dominic, Approved 14 February 1990, Reprinted October 2008, Maryknoll, New York 10545. See especially nos. 234, 262, and 286.

28. Rogers, "On Obedience," July 1931.

29. A transition style of governance had been in effect since 1969, when a regional governing board of three members assumed the responsibilities of the regional superior. Over time, as regional membership declined (due to aging, illness, death, transfers, withdrawals, and/or service at the Maryknoll Center), the members sought a more viable form of governance. They opted for an open style of shared leadership, dividing among themselves the responsibilities of the regional governing board.

30. Rogers, "Eve of Foundation Day," 13 February 1933, MMJR Papers, box 10, fold. 7, MMA.

31. Rogers, "Community Life," 28 January 1952, MMJR Papers, box 11, fold. 8, MMA.

32. Rogers, "Fraternal Charity," 29 September 1932, MMJR Papers, box 10, fold. 6, MMA.

33. Rogers, "Meditation—Morning of Elective Chapter," 2 January 1947, MMJR Papers, box 11, fold. 4, MMA. Emphasis added.

34. Rogers, "Obedience," 4 October 1940.

19. Nobility of Soul

1. Mother Mary Joseph Rogers, "Meditation—Eve of Foundation Day," 13 February 1933, MMJR [Mother Mary Joseph Rogers] Papers, box 10, fold. 7, Maryknoll Mission Archives, Maryknoll, NY (hereafter, MMA).

2. Rogers, "Maryknoll Spirit," 4 August 1940, MMJR Papers, box 10, fold. 8, MMA. Emphasis added. Found only on a small card, written in Mother Mary Joseph's own hand, 24 June 1935, the expression is "the saving grace of a *kindly* humor," instead of the more frequent quotation, "sense of humor." "Kindly" was retained in this quote because Mother Mary Joseph chose her words carefully, and "kindly" describes humor in a very gracious manner.

3. Rogers, "Meditation—Eve of Foundation Day."

4. The three conferences on the Maryknoll spirit were given 4 August 1930, 2 October 1932, and 4 August 1940. While a fourth, undated conference on the Maryknoll spirit does not begin with that quotation, Mother Mary Joseph brings it in toward the end of the talk, which constitutes an excellent summary of the spirit she sought to engender in the Congregation. The first three conferences listed may be found in MMJR Papers, box 10, folders 3, 6, and 8, respectively; the undated conference, in box 11, fold. 9, MMA. Lowell's poem is widely available.

5. Mother Mary Joseph Rogers, "Meditation—Eve of Foundation Day."

6. Ibid.

7. Ibid.

8. Rogers, "Fraternal Charity," 29 September 1932, MMJR Papers, box 10, fold. 6, MMA.

9. Ibid.

10. Rogers, "Community Life," 28 January 1952, MMJR Papers, box 11, fold. 8, MMA.

11. Rogers, "Chapter Talk," 6 April 1938, MMJR Papers, box 10, fold. 7, MMA.

12. Ibid.

20. *Ecce Ancilla Domini*

1. Mother Mary Joseph Rogers, letter, "My Dear Daughters in Christ," March 1930, MMJR [Mother Mary Joseph Rogers] Papers, box 3, fold. 2, Maryknoll Mission Archives, Maryknoll, NY (hereafter, MMA).

2. It was the Contemplative Community's custom in the early days to assume a special cloister name.

3. Rogers, "Feast of the Annunciation," 25 March 1933, MMJR Papers, box 10, fold. 7, MMA.

4. Ibid.

5. Rogers, "Behold the Handmaid of the Lord," 1941, MMJR Papers, box 11, fold. 1, MMA. Emphasis added.

6. Eugene LaVerdiere, "The Virgin's Name Was Mary" (Canfield, OH: Alba House Cassettes, 1998). The exposition of the text on the Annunciation in this theme is inspired by LaVerdiere's interpretation.

7. An *appearance* is not the same as an *apparition*. The latter refers to a visual image that can be described—for example, Lourdes—but does not, of itself, transform the visionary. An appearance refers to an interior transforming experience, like revelation. It cannot be described. To say that the angel appeared means that the angel made itself seen with the eyes of faith and/or experienced, and Mary was transformed. See Eugene LaVerdiere, *The New Testament in the Life of the Church* (Notre Dame, IN: Ave Maria Press, 1980), 6–7.

8. Rogers, "Feast of the Annunciation," 1933.

9. Ibid.

10. Ibid.

11. Rogers, "Feast of the Annunciation," 25 March 1942, MMJR Papers, box 11, fold. 1, MMA.

12. Ibid.

13. Rogers, "Meditation," 8 August 1943, MMJR Papers, box 11, fold. 2, MMA.

Bibliography

Primary Sources, in Maryknoll Mission Archives, Maryknoll, NY (MMA)

Callahan, Frank Rogers. "Rogers Family History, including Genealogy," 27 February 2005.

The Field Afar, especially volumes from 1912–24.

Hendricks, Barbara. "The Spiritual Heritage of Mother Mary Joseph," unpublished document written for Maryknoll Sisters, a collection of seven essays (1995).

Lane, John I. *Maryknoll Diary*. 15 January 1912—7 January 1915.

Rogers, Mother Mary Joseph. Conferences, retreats, and letters.

Tolan, Eunice, and Incarnata Farrelly, MM. *Maryknoll Distaff: History of the Maryknoll Sisters, 1912–1961.*

Vaughan, Laurence. *Chronicle of Notable Events in the History of Maryknoll according to Year 1860–1990*. Published by Maryknoll News. 1990.

Walsh, James Anthony. Conferences and letters.

Wholean, Mary Louise. *Teresian Diaries*. 5 volumes. 1912–16.

Secondary Sources

Anderson, Gerald H. "American Protestants in Pursuit of Missions: 1886–1986," *International Bulletin of Missionary Research* 12, no. 3 (1988).

Aschenbrenner, George, SJ. "The Spiritual Exercises of St. Ignatius Apostolic Spirituality, and Discernment." Eleven cassettes. St. Louis, 1976.

Bokenkotter, Thomas. *A Concise History of the Catholic Church*, rev. exp. ed. New York: Doubleday, 2004.

Brennan, Margaret R., IHM. *What Was There for Me Once*. Montreal: Novalis Publishing, 2009.

Breslin, Thomas A. *American Catholic China Missionaries, 1918–1941*. Ph.D. diss., University of Virginia (August 1972).

Briggs, Kenneth. *Double Crossed: Uncovering the Catholic Church's Betrayal of American Nuns*. New York: Doubleday, 2006.

De Mello, Anthony, SJ. *Seek God Everywhere*. New York: Image/Doubleday, 2010.

Dries, Angelyn. "The Foreign Mission Impulse of the American Catholic Church, 1893–1925," *International Bulletin of Missionary Research* 15, no. 2 (April 1991).

Kennedy, Camilla, MM. *To the Uttermost Parts of the Earth*. Maryknoll, NY: Maryknoll Sisters, 1980.

LaVerdiere, Eugene, SSS. *The New Testament in the Life of the Church*. Notre Dame, IN: Ave Maria Press, 1980.

———. "The Virgin's Name Was Mary." Canfield, OH: Alba House Cassettes, 1999.

Lowell, James Russell. "Yussouf." In *Complete Poetical Works of James Russell Lowell*. Boston and New York: Houghton, Mifflin and Company, The Riverside Press, Cambridge, 1899.

Lyons, Jeanne Marie, MM. *Maryknoll's First Lady*. New York: Dodd, Mead, and Company, 1964.

Newcomb, Clara Winifred. "Concerning Foreign Missionaries," *The Smith Alumnae Quarterly* 2, no. 2 (January 1911), 89–91.

Robert, Dana L. *American Women in Mission : A Social History of Their Thought and Practice*. Macon, GA: Mercer University Press, 1996.

———. "The Legacy of Arthur Tappan Pierson 1837–1911," *International Bulletin of Missionary Research* 8, no. 3 (1984).

———. "The Origin of the Student Volunteer Watchword: 'The Evangelization of the World in This Generation,'" *International Bulletin of Missionary Research* 10, no. 4 (1986).

Schneiders, Sandra. *New Wineskins: Re-imagining Religious Life*. New York: Paulist Press, 1986.

———. "Leadership and Spirituality in Postmodern Religious Congregations," keynote address to the Leadership Conference of Women Religious, 23 August 1997 (Rochester, NY).

Sheridan, Robert. *The Founders of Maryknoll*. Maryknoll, NY: The Catholic Foreign Mission Society of America, 1980.

Index

action (vs. contemplation), 84, 85–88
adaptability, 72–73
America, discussion in, on Rogers's education, 28–29
American Board of Commissioners for Foreign Missions, 55
Americanism, 62
Andover Theological Seminary, 55
Annunciation, 115–20
apostolic religious congregations, changes facing, 50–51
Arbuckle, Gerald, 83
Asia, upheavals in (late 1940s–early 1950s), 46–47
auxiliaries, perception of women as, 34–35

bandits (in China), 22–23, 25
Benedict XV, 15, 31
Berkeley, Xavier, 74
binary oppositions, 83
Borgmann, Henry, 13
Bréboeuf, Jean de, 61
Byrne, Patrick J., 23–24, 46

Cabrini, Frances, 61
Catherine of Siena, 112
Catholic Church, on the U.S. as mission territory, 61–62
Catholic education, 28–29
Catholic Foreign Mission Bureau, 62
Catholic Foreign Mission Society of America, 3, 7–8, 61, 84
Catholic Students' Mission Crusade, 62
Chang, Agneta, 46

charity, 91, 92–96
Chiang Kai-shek, 23
China
  ending of missions in, 46–47
  first mission assignments to, 21–22
  socio-political conditions in, when first Maryknollers arrived, 22–23
Chou en-Lai, 23
Church of San Stefano (Rome), 15
cloistered branch, of the Maryknoll Sisters, 31, 91
common good, 100–1, 113
compassion, 113
congruence, 82
Constitutions, creation of, 30–31
contemplation (vs. action), 84, 85–88
contemplative community, 31
contemplative spirit, cultivation of, 78–79
cooperation, 100, 102
Crisis of Christian Missions, The; or the Voice Out of the Cloud (Pierson), 56
criticism, destructive, 103
cultivation, 78–79, 98–99

Delaney, Fidelia, 19, 20, 27
de Mello, Anthony, 73
Devlin, Ruth, 17, 19
discrimination, anti-Catholic, 4
dispositions, 90
diversity, 89, 96
Dominic, Saint, 87, 112
Dominican Sisters of Sinsinawa (WI), 17, 19

155

Doyle, Alexander, 61
Duchesne, Philippine, 61
Dwyer, Mary, 8, 16

ejaculatory prayer, 80
Elliott, Walter, 61
Examen of Conscience, 81

Farley, John, 17
Field Afar, The, 7, 11, 62
    consuming time of novices, 16
    editorials in, calling for missionary
        service, 22
    Immaculate Heart Sisters hoping
        for end of, 16
    on Teresians becoming religious
        congregation, 12
Ford, Francis X., 24, 25–26, 32, 42,
    46, 72–73
foreign mission boards, proliferation
    of, 55–56
Foreign Mission Sisters of St. Dominic,
    official foundation of, 20
formation, for the early Teresians,
    13–14
Franciscan Missionaries of Mary, 13–
    14
Francis de Sales, 94
frankness. *See* honesty, fearless
fraternal charity, 94
Fumasoni-Biondi, Pietro, 73

General Association of Congrega-
    tional Churches, 55
generosity, 100, 101–2
Gibbons, James, 7–8
God
    offering daily thoughts, words,
        and acts to, 80
    presence of, 78–82, 99
gossip, 95
governance
    horizontal, 104
    participative, 103, 113
    traditional, in religious orders, 104

Handly, John, 6
Hanscom, Elizabeth Deering, 6, 64
Hawthorne, Nathaniel, 9
Hawthorne (NY), site for new mis-
    sion seminary, 8
Hayes, Patrick Joseph, 21
Hendricks, Barbara, 83
Henry VIII, 112
*History of the Student Volunteer
    Movement for Foreign Mis-
    sions* (Mott), 57
Holy Childhood Association, 5
home mission, 55
honesty, fearless, 83, 110, 112–13
Hong Kong, 24, 36–37

individuality, 97–99

Japan, 23–24
Japanese Americans, internment of,
    39
Japanese immigrants, work with, 21
jealousy, 93
Jogues, Isaac, 61

Korea, 25, 46
Kunkel, Hyacinth, 40
Kuomintang (KMT), 22–23

Lathrop, Alphonsa (Rose Hawthorne),
    9
Latin America, 39–40
leadership, horizontal style of, 51
l'Incarnation, Marie de, 61
listening, deep, 104
localized missions, 61
Louis IX, 112
Lourdes, 14
Lowell, James Russell, 111

Manifest Destiny, 56
Mao Tse-tung, 23
Maria Teresa, Sister, 89
martyrdom, 15, 62–63
Maryknoll Fathers and Brothers, 3

Maryknoll Mission Movement
  founding of, 7–8
  beginnings of, 9–11
  spirit of, 14
  during World War II, 38–40
Maryknoll (NY), move to, 10–11
Maryknoll Sisters Congregation
  apostolic style of, 72–74
  benefitting from discussion in *America* about Catholic education, 29
  called to apostolic vocation, 35
  cloister of, 15, 31, 91
  Constitutions of, incorporating mission policy, 71
  daily work of, 102–3
  first groups of novices, 21–22
  General Chapter of 1925, 27–28
  General Chapter of 1931, 30–31
  growth of, during Rogers's life, 50
  ideal qualities of, 42
  individuality encouraged within, 97–99
  limited communication among, during World War II era, 35–36
  making financial appeals through parishes, 29
  mission policy of, 68–74
  motto of, 116
  openness of, to women of other cultures, 89
  origins of, 3
  participative governance, 103
  qualities desired in, 111
  racism within, recognition of, 89–90
  responding to Vatican II, 51
  responsibility for, 101
  sent two-by-two in China, 26
  simplifying the prayer life of, 43
McKenna, Mary Paul, 24, 25
McMahon, Mary Lumena, 27
McNicholas, John T., 16, 17, 19

mission
  formation for, as lifetime process, 71–72
  virtues for, 82
missionary movement, U.S., history of, 55–56
mission diaries, of the World War II era, 35–36
Motherhouse, 29–30
Mott, John, 57
Mount Hermon 100, 57
Mount Hermon Summer Conference (1881), 56–57

native sisterhoods, forming, priority of, 30–31
naturalness, 99
nobility, 111–14
Nun in the World, The (Suenens), 51

obedience, 104–10
Ossining (NY), purchasing property in, for Maryknoll's permanent home, 9–10

Particular Examen, 80–81
perpetual adoration, 15, 36
Philippines, 37
Pierson, Arthur Tappan, 56–57
Pius X, 15, 62
Pius XII, 50, 51
Plummer, Bridget Josephine Kennedy, 4
Plummer, William Gardner, 4
postulation, 42–44
prayer, 15–16, 80, 81. *See also* contemplation
Price, Thomas Frederick, 7–8, 18, 19–20, 61, 63
Protestants, missionary movement among, 55–56

racism, 89–90
recollection, 81–82
religious orders, governance in, 104

Rogers, Abraham, 3–4, 7

Rogers, Josie Plummer, 4

Rogers, Mary Dunn, 3

Rogers, Mary James, 36

Rogers, Mary Josephine (Mollie)

appointed first prioress, 21

aversion of, to religious life, 59

balancing religious observance and work, 16

becoming mother founder, 44

becoming Walsh's daily collaborator, 66

binary oppositions in writings of, 83

birth of, 3

buying property at Ossining, 9–10

called to mission, 7, 58–60

calling General Chapter for 1946, 42

caring for Mary Joseph Wholean, 17, 18

childhood of, 4–5

commentary on the Annunciation, 116–20

commitment of, to the church, 5

communicating simplicity, 77

concerned with overburdening the community, 86

concluding words of, as mother general, 44

conferences with the Sisters, 14, 71

contributing to *Field Afar*, 7, 62

determining plans during World War II, 38

on diversity, 89–91, 96

down-to-earth nature of, 73–74

early awareness of church's foreign missionary activity, 4–5

education of, 4–6

elected first mother general, 28

encouraging individuality among the Sisters, 97–99

establishing financial base for the Sisters, 29

eulogizing Fidelia Delaney, 27

extending mission vision to U.S. minority groups, 40

final days and death of, 48–49

final letters of, 48

final vow as Maryknoll Sister, 25

first meeting with Walsh, 6–7

first visitations of, 68

formulating a mission policy, 30, 68–74

General Chapter of 1937, 34–35

giving retreats as mother founder, 44–45

health of, 39

influences on, 15–16, 55, 77–78, 84–85

least theologically prepared among the Maryknoll founders, 68

letter to Walsh, written while at Smith College, 64–65

on life in community, 92–96

listening to God's voice, 77

at Maryknoll Sanitorium, 44

meeting Wholean, 8

move to Valley Park (MO) novitiate, 44–45

negotiating skills of, 4

on obedience, 104–10

offering bold and dynamic vision to young Catholics, 63

path of, to Maryknoll, 64–66

permanent return of, to Hawthorne, 9

placed in charge at Hawthorne, 10

preparing for General Chapter of 1931, 30

presenting a session at the Smith College Mission Study Classes, 57–58

recalling collaboration with Walsh, 33

receiving honorary doctorate from Smith College, 45–46

recognizing tension between contemplation and action, 85–88

reflecting on challenges of mission work in China, 27

reflecting on Teresians' direction toward religious life, 20

reflecting on World War II years, 41

relying on God's presence, 78–82

return to Motherhouse (1950), 45

on seeing other Sisters as God sees them, 91–92

starting the Maryknoll Sisters, 3

suffering a severe stroke, 47

transferring to teach for the Boston city schools, 7

travel to Europe with Julia Ward, 14–15

unanimous reelection of (1946), 42–44

visiting Hawaii and Asia (1940), 36–37

working at Smith after graduation, 6

Rogers, Patrick Henry, 3

Rome, Rogers and Ward in, 15

Ryan, Joan Marie, 46

Sapienti Consilio (Pius X), 62

Second Vatican Council, 51

secretaries

becoming religious, 12–20

Teresa of Avila as model for, 12

self-will, 99

Serra, Junipero, 61

Shea, Margaret (Sister Gemma), 10, 21

Shea, Nora, 8, 9

silence, 81, 97

single-mindedness, 82

Sister Formation Movement, 50–51

Sisters of the Company of Mary (Blue Nuns), 15

Sisters Servants of the Immaculate Heart of Mary, 14, 16–17

Smith College

Catholic students marginalized at, 6

mission study classes at, 64–65

missionary spirit at, 57–60

Society for the Propagation of the Faith, 5

Spellman, Francis, 43

Student Volunteer Movement for Foreign Missions (SVM), 5, 57, 62

Suenens, Leon Joseph, 51

Sullivan, Sara, 8

Sun Yat-sen, 22–23

superiors

new titles for, 109

Rogers's counseling of, 106

Tarpey, Columba, 44, 49

Teresa of Avila, 12, 13, 77–78, 84–85

Teresian Diary, 12

Teresians, 12

becoming a religious community, 12–20

enrolled as Dominican tertiaries, 16

invalid novitiate of, 16

petitioning to become a religious congregation, 17, 18–19

required to be separate from the Maryknoll Society, 19

Theissling, Louis, 20

transparency, 82, 114

United States, minority groups in, mission for, 40

Vénard, Théophane, 63

vespers, 85–86

vows, maturing in, 109

Walsh, James Anthony, 3, 6–7, 42, 61–62

buying property at Ossining, 9–10

early description of Maryknoll beginnings, 11

eulogy for Wholean, 17–18
giving equal priority to home missions, 62–63
guiding Teresians in becoming a religious community, 13–14
holding Rogers up as a model, 84
illness and death of, 32–33
offering bold and dynamic vision to young Catholics, 63
ordination of, as titular bishop of Siene, 31–32
placing Rogers in charge at Hawthorne, 10
plans for setting up a foreign mission seminary in America, 7–8

printing student letter from Rogers in *Field Afar*, 65
recognizing Rogers's leadership skills, 8–9
responding to letter from Rogers while at Smith, 65–66
Walsh, James Edward, 20, 34–35
Ward, Julia, 14–15
Wholean, Mary Louise, 8, 12, 13, 17–18
women, role of, in mission, 34–35
World Parliament of Religions, 61
World War II, 35–41

Xavier, Francis, 87